W9-AEO-797

6
99
c. 2

# THE TOOLBOX FOR THE MIND:

## Finding and Implementing Creative Solutions in the Workplace

**Also available from ASQ Quality Press**

*Critical SHIFT:*
*The Future of Quality*
*in Organizational Performance*
Lori L. Silverman with Annabeth L. Propst

*Success through Quality:*
*Support Guide for the Journey*
*to Continuous Improvement*
Timothy J. Clark

*101 Good Ideas:*
*How to Improve Just about Any Process*
Karen Bemowski and Brad Stratton, editors

*Creativity, Innovation, and Quality*
Paul E. Plsek

*The Balanced Scorecard:*
*Translating Strategy into Action*
Robert S. Kaplan and David P. Norton

*Images of Organization:*
*The Executive Edition*
Gareth Morgan

*Leading the Way to Competitive Excellence:*
*The Harris Mountaintop Case Study*
William A Levinson, editor

*Lead with Vision:*
*Manage the Strategic Challenge*
John L. Thompson

To request a complimentary catalog of ASQ Quality Press publications, call 800-248-1946

# THE TOOLBOX FOR THE MIND:

## Finding and Implementing Creative Solutions in the Workplace

D. Keith Denton, Ph.D.

With contributions from
Rebecca A. Denton

ASQ Quality Press
Milwaukee, Wisconsin

*The Toolbox for the Mind: Finding and Implementing Creative Solutions in the Workplace*
D. Keith Denton with contributions from Rebecca A. Denton

## Library of Congress Cataloging-in-Publication Data

Denton, D. Keith.
   The toolbox for the mind : finding and implementing creative
solutions in the workplace / by D. Keith Denton with contributions
from Rebecca A. Denton.
        p.   cm.
      Includes bibliographical references and index.
      ISBN 0-87389-448-0 (alk. paper)
      1. Creative ability in business.    2. Problem solving.    3. Product
management.   I. Denton, Rebecca A.   II. Title
   HD53.D46      1999
   153.4'3--dc21                                        99-18724
                                                        CIP

© 1999 by ASQ

All rights reserved. No part of this book may be reproduced in any form or by any means, electronic, mechanical, photocopying, recording, or otherwise, without the prior written permission of the publisher.

10 9 8 7 6 5 4 3 2 1

ISBN 0-87389-448-0

Acquisitions Editor:  Ken Zielske
Project Editor:  Annemieke Koudstaal
Production Coordinator:  Shawn Dohogne

ASQ Mission: The American Society for Quality advances individual and organizational performance excellence worldwide by providing opportunities for learning, quality improvement, and knowledge exchange.

Attention: Bookstores, Wholesalers, Schools and Corporations:
ASQ Quality Press books, videotapes, audiotapes, and software are available at quantity discounts with bulk purchases for business, educational, or instructional use. For information, please contact ASQ Quality Press at 800-248-1946, or write to ASQ Quality Press, P.O. Box 3005, Milwaukee, WI 53201-3005.

To place orders or to request a free copy of the ASQ Quality Press Publications Catalog, including ASQ membership information, call 800-248-1946.  Visit our web site at http://www.asq.org.

Printed in the United States of America

 Printed on acid-free paper

**American Society for Quality**

Quality Press
611 East Wisconsin Avenue
Milwaukee, Wisconsin 53202
Call toll free 800-248-1946
http://www.asq.org
http://standardsgroup.asq.org

# DEDICATION

To my greatest creative enterprise,
my daughter, Taylor Logan Denton.

DEDICATION

# CONTENTS

### Section I:   Creativity and Innovation
### CHAPTER 1

### Defining Creativity   1

### CHAPTER 2

### The Creativity Zone: Between Order and Chaos   11

## CHAPTER 5

## Section II:   Using Creativity Techniques and Knowledge Tools
## CHAPTER 6

## CHAPTER 7

### In the Zone: The Panda Principle's Basics of Product and Process Innovation   73

## CHAPTER 8

### Risk Taking, Innovation, and Product Development   81

## CHAPTER 9

### Developing a Creative Workplace: Managing the Direction—Not the Details 93

## CHAPTER 10

### Innovation through Technology: A Historical Lesson 103

# LIST OF ILLUSTRATIONS

# PREFACE

*Toolbox for the Mind* is a different kind of book. It aims to help you find innovative solutions to today's problems using an interdisciplinary approach. The book examines how to think creatively and come up with innovative solutions through a variety of *tools*. These tools, principles, or guidelines are placed throughout the chapters to highlight essential aspects. For instance, chapter 1 stresses the importance of being able to ask good questions as an essential component of thinking creatively. A critical step in this process is to *ASK WHY BEFORE ASKING HOW.*

Some involve adopting a different perspective on a problem and how to solve it. Others ask you to approach your task in a different way. Some of these tool boxes may be familiar; others are quite unique. More familiar ones might be the need to *PROVIDE CONTINUAL FEEDBACK.* Others are unlikely to have been seen before and involve the need to *VALUE MUTATIONS* or to *CREATE MANAGEABLE ADVERSITY* and *SEEK ADAPTIVE CHALLENGES.* These tools can and have helped individuals, groups, and large organizations find novel solutions and produce dramatic innovations. Chapters within the book contain numerous other practical and applied techniques. The last chapter includes a collection of techniques and exercises that either were mentioned in earlier chapters or ones that complement the ones already demonstrated.

*Toolbox for the Mind* is divided into three major sections. The first section of chapters examines the process of creativity and innovative thinking by exploring what we call your *creativity zone.* Entering the zone helps you find new perspectives on your problem or helps you approach a problem from a different viewpoint. Chapters 3 and 4 provide you with a wide range of ways to help you find these new solutions.

The toolbox can provide some new perspectives because it is interdisciplinary. It draws on various disciplines including biology, physics, and history to suggest a wide range of ways for solving problems. For instance, chapter 5 discussed Darwinianism and evolutionary biology as a way of finding new solutions. The concepts of manageable adversity and adaptive challenges are the result of a transfer of knowledge from one discipline to management.

The second section of the book is a how-to approach. It is designed to provide you with ideas for improving product, process, and services by using some of the knowledge acquired in earlier chapters. Tools like: BEING SENSITIVE TO SMALL CHANGES, SEPARATING RESPONSIBILITY AND ACCOUNTABILITY and USING BROAD BASIC RULES were all distilled from knowledge acquired in previous chapters.

One of many examples of using some of these tools involved Kodak managers in its consumer imaging business who asked, "What if we could make cameras that were disposable?" or when Nike asked, "Would consumers pay over $100 (three times the price of an acceptable alternative) for a high performance athletic shoe?" These are good examples of visualizing an ideal future by framing a question. They then worked backwards to the present day to determine what was required for this future state (Krinsky 1997). Other examples, too numerous to mention, show the practical application of these techniques.

The final section is devoted to how to successfully implement innovative solutions. Tools within this area, among others, include: MANAGING THE DIRECTION, focusing on RESULTS-ORIENTED OBJECTIVES and KNOWING YOUR PRIORITIES AND TRADE-OFFS to mention just a few. The primary purpose is to both get your creative ideas implemented and encourage groups and organizations to continue to change and be competitive.

It was Abraham Maslow who was reported to have once said, "If the only tool you have is a hammer, you tend to treat everything as a nail." The world is full of nails, but not every problem can be solved by a hammer or by the common way you solve problems. Often we must find new solutions to today's problems. This book aims to give you a toolbelt full of new tools to bring to these old and future problems.

Krinsky, Robert. 1997. When world's collide: The uneasy fusion of strategy and innovation. *Strategy and Leadership* 25, no. 4 (July–August): 9.

# ACKNOWLEDGMENTS

This book, as any, is very much a joint effort. There are numerous people, published and otherwise, who have had an important influence, but two are noteworthy. The entire text has had many revisions. Anita Looney is largely responsible for the typing and frequent editing. The job of producing the text was made much easier by her truly unlimited dedication to perfection. It is truly a rare ingredient.

Finally, I would like to acknowledge a contributing author, Rebecca A. Denton. She not only provided frequent insights into the concepts of creativity and how our minds work but also edited, revised, and improved large sections of the book. I have no doubt that the final product was greatly enhanced through her analysis and suggestions.

ACKNOWLEDGMENTS

# CHAPTER 1

# Defining Creativity

## INTRODUCTION

This chapter examines how you can become more creative. Different personalities express their creativity in different ways. Creativity can flower in structured as well as less-structured environments. All of us can become more creative, can do things differently, and can think in contrary ways. The key is in formulating problems and asking insightful questions, including the following:

- First ask why not—before you ask how.
- Challenge your commonsense assumptions.
- Post the correct problem and ask questions in a straightforward manner.

Change continues to accelerate and affects society and the workplace in subtle and often unimaginable ways. We have evolved into a global community in which there is fierce competition and often unpredictable, even chaotic changes. Once new products remained on the market for five to seven years so companies could get back their initial investment. Today compressed life cycles require bigger revenue hits because products are on the market for a shorter time. For example, a new prescription drug needs to turn a profit within five years of launch before it is replaced by a more effective remedy (Krinsky 1997). Knowledge and intellectual capabilities are the critical competitive differences.

Our creative solutions to existing products, processes, and services will continue to be the only true competitive advantages. Arie de Geus, former planner at Royal Dutch/Shell, once observed, "The ability to learn faster than our competitors may be our only sustainable competitive weapon" (Harari 1996).

Often, though, too little effort is given to encourage creativity and innovative thinking. Paul Reichmann, one of Canada's top business executives, has said that liberal arts graduates are better prepared for business in today's world than MBAs.

The liberal arts major has learned to think freely. Lee Iacocca once said, "MBAs know everything and understand nothing." He was referring to the fact that MBAs have formulas for everything, but these are often useless in an age in which creativity and innovation are most needed (Zelinski 1989). People often grow up in uncreative environments. They go to school where more effort is placed on repetition and formulas for problems than on approaching solutions in innovative ways. It becomes all too easy to believe that we are not creative.

> ## ALWAYS ASK YOURSELF WHY—RATHER THAN HOW

Describing yourself as uncreative is perhaps the single greatest obstacle to innovation. One study found, for instance, that the main difference between creative and less creative people is that creative people think they are creative and less creative people think they are not (Swanson 1997). It can become a self-fulfilling prophecy that imposes imaginary limits on ourselves. Lauren Swanson, an associate professor of marketing, believes that all people are creative and that creativity can be nurtured through development of creative habits, including **thinking contrary.** Her advice is if their consensus is yes, then ask "Why not no?"

If the trend is to add more products, functions, or steps, then ask, "Why not fewer?" An example of a good *why* question versus *how-to* questions was the one posed by Peter Drucker in the 1970s. He asked executives, "If you weren't already in this business, would you enter it today?" (Sherman 1993). Many managers realized the answer was no. But the reason it never occurred to them was that they had been too busy asking "How can we improve?" or other how-to questions. Always challenge the obvious and ask, "Is it really obvious or not?" See all problems as opportunities for creative solutions. Find more than one solution. That's what this book is about—new ways of thinking and new approaches to problems. Chapters 3 and 4 in particular will explore more fully how to think differently, in opposite ways, and how to come up with novel solutions. Chapter 5 will show how to generate more creative solutions using a Darwinian approach, and chapter 8 will examine more fully how to ask good why questions. However creativity is more than finding new perspectives or thinking in unique ways. It involves having a particular mindset toward taking risk and making mistakes.

# FINDING WELLSPRINGS OF CREATIVITY

Although it is true that certain people display a stronger tendency toward creativity, it is equally true that all people have creative potential. As William E. Coyne, Senior Vice President of Research and Development at 3M, says, "You can't ask people to have unique visions and march in lockstep. Some people are very precise, detail-oriented people . . . and others are fuzzy thinkers and visionaries . . ." (Coyne 1996). He goes on to say that different kinds of innovation require different personalities. Some of their customers require very precise solutions. Other problems are broader and that is when they need a more open, visionary mind-set.

Coyne's comments are backed up by Charles Prather's research, which shows that most people are creative in one form or another. Rather it is more of a problem of finding the right environment for your creativity. He says some people feel more comfortable operating in a more structured work environment. It is what this book refers to as *below the (creative) zone* (see chapter 6). Prather says these people are more comfortable operating *within the box*. They like structure, rules, and organization and use their creative skills to make an existing system work better. Accounting, insurance, pharmacy or administration might tend to attract these kinds of people (Capowski 1994).

The outside the box types like to try out new ideas and concepts. These types of creative personalities produce more innovative and useful suggestions when they are under noncontrolling supervision. Coyne says these types of people often require a tolerance for mistakes. They are the ones that produce more original and useful suggestions when their jobs are more complex (Tabak 1997). The message seems to be that creative people are everywhere; it's a matter of matching personalities to jobs and supervisors. It is also a matter of reaching for your creative potential.

Michael Eisner, Disney's CEO, was discussing how we can all find hidden depths and new wellsprings of creativity. He mentioned a retreat that top Disney management attended that was given by a husband–wife team who teach at the Harvard Medical School. Their talk focused on the need for people to connect with their emotional depths. The presenters said that being connected to these emotional depths was critical to releasing our most powerful and creative forces. The opposite of this is being disconnected and losing touch with fundamental aspects of who we are.

Eisner said he was especially struck by the point that fear of criticism and lack of acceptance are primary reasons why people so often censor their feelings and intuitions and shut down their depths. For him, it explained much about the difference between those who are truly creative and those who are somehow blocked, limited, or superficial. He believes that this has a very practical creative value. People who produce their best and most creative work do so when they are not afraid to take risks or to endure criticism, embarrassment, or even failure (Eisner 1996, 8). Creativity, for Eisner, begins with *risk taking*. It means being able to trust your deepest intuitive feelings and instincts, which may mean even overriding contrary research, peer pressure, conventional wisdom, or intimidation.

Everyone is and can be more creative, but Eisner is right when he believes that creative people have a tendency to display particular attributes. Studies show these people not only have preferences for complexity and novelty, the same studies confirm what Disney might refer to as expressing irrational impulses. Most people bend to peer pressure or conventional wisdom. **Doing things differently** and being unafraid to take risks are hallmarks of the very creative (Coates and Jarrott 1994).

## ENCOURAGE PASSION AND RISK TAKING

A young researcher at 3M named Lew Leht demonstrates some of these personality characteristics. He was a key developer of 3M's first surgical drapes. He remained convinced of their potential even when they failed initially in the marketplace. He remained convinced even after his supervisors told him that they were losing money on the product and wanted to get rid of it. Leht did agree to kill the project just as soon as the inventory was depleted.

What he neglected to tell the factory was that he had built up a substantial inventory! The product eventually became a solid performer for 3M and the first in a long line of health care products. To 3M's credit, Lew Leht was not punished for his insubordination. In fact, he worked his way up through the ranks to eventually become chairman of the board. When Leht did become chairman, he did not try to make the labs bend to his will. Rather he believed it was better to ask forgiveness than permission (Coyne 1996). Chapter 8 gives specific suggestions on how to tolerate failure and risk taking so that innovative behavior can occur in individuals, groups, and organizations.

# INSIGHTFUL QUESTIONS

Creative personalities may vary, but one absolute essential is the need for insight. Doris Wallace notes that insight is important because it serves to reorganize thoughts by integrating previously unrelated elements into a new harmonious whole. Insight often occurs after earlier struggles and often entails an abrupt reorganization of previous thinking (Wallace 1991). Insight is thinking that reaches out beyond what is known and involves putting known elements together to form new ideas and products. It involves observation, experience, and knowledge that are put together in unique ways to produce novel insights.

It is often extremely difficult to be able to think in novel ways and make the leap from what is known to that which might be unknown. Our common sense tends to tell us that anything that is different from what we know is nonsense. Imagine or remember, if you are old enough, a market and a time when carbon paper was used instead of copiers. People used carbon paper to make copies at the same time as they typed. It would have challenged common sense to use a new machine to do this task. It would seem to be adding a new step. Imagine someone saying, "Now let me get this straight—if we buy this machine to make copies—something we already can do—and it's in a different place than our typewriter? Hmm."

Few would be able to see the future of this new product. It would not simply be used to make a copy of the original like carbon paper did but rather to make copies of copies of copies. This technology even evolved a whole new set of procedures and work practices that have changed the way we work. It became easier to share information. The process probably started out gradually and then, like the Internet is doing today, quickly restructured what was and was not possible.

However, the copiers would probably not have had the rapid impact it did without some marketing innovation. Instead of trying to sell to a hesitant market, Haloid (later renaming itself Xerox) bought the patent and decided to make its return from use fees. Every time someone made a copy, Xerox made money. It allowed people to take a chance on a machine with minimum cost and risk (Brown n. d.).

## CHALLENGE YOUR COMMONSENSE ASSUMPTIONS

Becoming more creative begins by asking yourself, "Can I imagine any other way?" It begins by focusing yourself on one aspect of a problem and asking, "How can we (solve that) so it is not a problem?" Some have suggested that the most important part of this problem-solving process is to properly define the problem or more properly *post the correct problem* which then allows for solutions to be discovered (Nonoka and Kenney 1995). A good illustration of this point was provided by the Japanese company Canon when in the fall of 1970 it developed plain paper copier (PPC) technology. In 1979 Canon introduced a PPC that used completely original technology and did not violate any of Xerox's over 600 patents, but by 1982 demand had leveled off for PPC products. Office saturation appeared to be complete.

This is the point that separated Canon from less innovative competitors. Instead of viewing their market as mature, they challenged this commonsense assumption. They began to think of their market not in terms of whether a firm has a copier, but rather *in terms of individual offices.* This was a new perspective, one that others had not visualized, and this new viewpoint convinced them that the market was much larger than originally envisioned. If small offices could use a copier, so could small businesses, and maybe even home use was possible. Even large firms with a PPC might be interested in a desk-side model.

# FORMULATING THE PROBLEM

Insight and creativity come from a willingness to challenge our assumptions or common sense about what is and why it is so. A good example of challenging the obvious comes from Rhonda Holley, a flight attendant at Southwest Airlines. She wrote to the company executives and suggested that they should remove the logo from the white plastic bags used for collecting trash at the end of the flight. Her argument was that nobody really cares about the logo on a trash bag. Management decided that this was a good idea. By using trash bags without logos, Southwest saved $300,000 per year (Freiberg and Freiberg 1996, 130). Creative people like Rhonda ask questions that frame problems so there are opportunities to innovate. These questions should be in straightforward language in order to encourage inventive solutions. Phrases like "develop a more efficient electric automobile" is straight and to the point. It is easy though to get lost in the details.

Consider the following situation facing General Motors when they wanted to create a new concept car. The initial definition of the problem they faced was to take a standard automobile then reduce the amount of energy it could carry on board equal to half a gallon of gasoline. Now add almost a ton of dead weight in the form of 26 lead-acid batteries, but don't sacrifice air conditioning, power windows, CD player, rear-window defogger, or any other amenities. Oh, yes, and make it handle tight to the road like a sports coupe. How would you like to solve that problem? Well, that was what innovator Kenneth R. Baker, Vice President of Research and Development at General Motors, was facing.

His solution was to frame a simple, straightforward problem and not to buy into the old, excessively detailed definition of the problem. It was too specific, too confining. Creative insights often begin by challenging assumptions about the problem. He said you can't just start with a standard automobile and remove the guts and plug in electric parts. Instead, they needed an entirely new automobile. They started challenging their assumptions about the real problem—not imaginary problems they needed to solve. They surveyed driving habits, which suggested that a car with a limited range would serve 90 percent of driving needs. A small two-seater with a range of only 70 to 90 miles between rechargings could be trimmed by hundreds of pounds and still be a good second car for normal commuting, shopping, and driving kids to school (1997 Discovery Awards).

With their definition of their problem simplified, it then came down to a simple question for efficiency. The concept car called the Impact is lightweight, has a highly aerodynamic shape on a 290-pound aluminum frame and accelerates from zero to 60 in less than nine seconds. It matches the performance of the BMW 318I but with zero emissions.

Innovation began with reframing a problem in a more straightforward manner. Innovation solution often begins with phrases like the following:

- "How to improve . . ."
- "How to eliminate . . ."
- "How to simplify . . ."
- "How do we improve customer service while still . . ."
- "How do we break down the walls separating . . ."

The importance of problem formulation in successful creative problem solving cannot be overstated. An old adage says it all, "a problem well-defined is half-solved." A client wanted to "minimize the *percentage* of scrap" in a cutting process. The client had an effective computer routine for generating and evaluating cutting-stock situations and then computing the percentage of scrap. It was a fairly straightforward application of implicit enumeration. However, new solutions arise by changing the definition to "minimizing the *actual amount* of scrap." Immediately, the firm noticed that they were using different-sized stock to generate cutting patterns. A small percentage of scrap on a large piece of stock generated a large amount of scrap! Changing from control *percentages* to *actual amount* made the solution obvious (Volkema 1995).

## IMPLEMENTING CREATIVITY AT XEROX

The reason for asking good questions is to be able to see the whole of a change rather than the pieces of it. That is what Xerox tried to do when they made a change. A transition team was charged with identifying the key characteristics that would be needed to help Xerox remain competitive, which they called Xerox 2000. The team, over a nine-month period, designed detailed changes that would be needed to be taken to meet Xerox's 2000 strategy (Brown and Walton 1993).

They began the process by first doing a reality check. The team recognized the danger of making assumptions and wanted to see what was actually being done rather than what was being said. They wanted to know "how do our people actually behave" rather than what they were supposed to do. Such a reality check is often disturbing, but almost always useful.

Xerox's management was not only interested in where most of the organization was headed but also where the stragglers were going. They wanted to discover divergent behavior, radicalism, and innovation, as well as their normal culture. When they did find radicalism, they hired anthropologists to take a closer look so they could understand the big picture rather than simply accepting what people said was happening. This is one of the key reasons for hiring *outsiders* or other consultants. Once the anthropologists were inside these pockets of innovation, they were then withdrawn and were asked to summarize their insights.

Analysis of six such experiments around the world brought some interesting insights. They learned not only about the organization as a whole, but also about why there were isolated pockets of innovation rather than widespread areas. Xerox discovered what they called the *double blind,* a set of beliefs that were self-canceling and self-sealing (Brown and Walton 1993, 6). For instance, they found out, to no one's surprise, that Xerox personnel deeply believe in teamwork (for example, Team Xerox) as a means of achieving greater competitiveness. Although teamwork was highly valued, they also discovered that the culture had a strong hero-worshiping mentality, which gave special status to the superstar. Two such viewpoints are not only interrelated but also are self-canceling because hero worship runs counter to a team-based culture.

Xerox knew they would need to be more than simply a copier company if they hoped to survive in the twenty-first century. They felt changes were needed in order for them to remain competitive. As long as employees thought of themselves as working for a copier company, things would remain the same. They would keep coming up with new technology to make working with documents easier and more efficient or slowly grow extinct. They knew that making a small change in who you are would change everything.

## REDEFINING YOURSELF ENCOURAGES INNOVATION

Xerox changed the definition of who they were (see Exercise #2 in Chapter 14 for how to go about this process ) about halfway through their change process. Rather than thinking of themselves as a *document-processing company,* they began to see themselves as simply a *document company.* At first this might seem like a simple change. They only eliminated one word, but the people on the team began to change their attitudes and perspectives. The new focus at Xerox was to begin to associate themselves more with *documents* than with processing those documents. With this new perspective came a new mission. They would attempt to focus their people more on creating value by enabling documents to be an integrating force in and across corporations (Brown and Walton 1993, 7).

Previously, Xerox had concentrated on creating new processing technologies for eliminating waste and making it easier to work with documents. Now, they had a new innovative concept and began to concentrate on *live time* as well as eliminating dead time. Before they focused on eliminating waste, now they were innovating by thinking of creating value.

They began to ask fundamental questions about what they were doing and, most importantly, from a creativity standpoint, *why.* The team eventually came up with 17 interrelated and adaptive characteristics they would use to define what they wanted to achieve. The criteria they chose were not particularly unique and included tenants like reduced time to market and simplifying the organization. This analysis caused them to reorganize divisions based on distinct decision-makers who would buy a group of products. The team spent a great deal of time clarifying each new function that would exist at each level of the company and what type of people they wanted to fill those positions.

Additional ways of empowering your creative mind through problem formulation and redefining the definition of the problem are described in Exercise #2 (Management-by-the-Fundamental Question) in chapter 14.

# SUMMARY

The world will always need creative people, but it seems especially critical in today's ever-changing economic climate. All too often we doom ourselves by believing we are not creative. Nothing could be further from the truth. To reach your creative potential takes both the right environment and a questioning and open approach to new information.

The entire creative process begins by asking fundamental, simple questions that challenge our common sense. The more creative of us have a lot more respect for nonsense. We also have a willingness to take risk. Even though some people may be more predisposed to take risk, to challenge convention, and to ask clear, simple questions, that does not limit any of us from developing more creative minds. Ultimately, creativity asks us to be open to new information, new perspectives, and making new connections. We now know that the brain continues to rewire itself and that it is not simply hardware and software. Knowledge for us, unlike the computer, really does change the circuits. New knowledge and new perspectives help us learn to think creatively and differently. It does require us to give up our status quo attitude and to put ourselves in a state of flux through which we can absorb and grow new connections. Chapter 2 more fully describes this *zone of creativity* and helps you to identify how much chaos or stability will be needed for you and your organization.

# REFERENCES

1997 Discovery Awards. 1997. *Discover,* July, 65.

Brown, John Seely. n.d. Seeing differently: Insights on innovation. Pamphlet, p. XI.

Brown, John Seely, and Elise Walton. 1993. Reenacting the corporation. *Planning Review* (September/October): 5–8.

Capowski, Genevieve. 1994. What flavor is in your ice cream cone? *Management Review* 83, no. 12 (December): 7.

Coates, Joseph F., and Jennifer Jarrott. 1994. Workplace creativity. *Employee Relations Today* 21, no. 1 (spring): 19.

Coyne, William E. 1996. Building a tradition of innovation. *UK Innovation Lecture,* 5 May, 5–9.

Eisner, Michael. 1996. Speech to Chicago Executives Club. Chicago, Ill., 19 April, 8.

Freiberg, Kevin, and Jackie Freiberg. 1996. *Nuts! Southwest Airlines' crazy recipe for business and personal success.* Austin, Tex.: Bard Press.

Harari, Oren. 1996. Mind Matters. *Management Review* 85, no. 1 (January): 49.

Krinsky, Robert. 1997. "When worlds collide: the uneasy fusion of strategy and innovation." *Strategy and Leadership* 25, no. 4 (July-August): 38-39.

Nonoka, Ikujiro, and Martin Kenney. 1995. Towards a new theory of innovation management. *IEEE Engineering Management Review* 23, no. 2: 2.

Sherman, Stratford. 1993. Are you as good as the best in the world. *Fortune,* 13 December (reprint).

Swanson, Lauren. 1997. A Chinese view of birthing and growing ideas. *Marketing News* 31, no. 7 (31 March): 17.

Tabak, Filiz. 1997. Employee creative performance: What makes it happen? *Academy of Management Executive* 11, no. 1: 120.

Volkema, Roger J. 1995. Creativity in MS/OR: Managing the process of formulating the problem. *Interfaces* 25 (May–June): 81.

Wallace, Doris B. 1991. The genesis and microgenesis of sudden insight in the creation of literature. *Creativity Research Journal* 4, no. 1: 43, 48.

Zelinski, Ernest J. 1989. Creativity training for business. *Canadian Manager/Manager Canadian* (summer): 24.

# CHAPTER 2

# The Creativity Zone:
# Between Order and Chaos

## INTRODUCTION

Creativity depends on two great universal forces; one is **order,** the other is **chaos.** Creative minds and organizations must not be quite stable nor quite chaotic. Each of these forces can be best understood and managed through something called chaos theory and the sciences of complexity.

This chapter shows how creativity occurs when we are somewhat *out of sync* with our environment. This condition requires that we

- Have an open system rather than a closed one
- Use rules of thumb, rather than rules
- Match our creative needs to our environment
- Know our Innovative IQ

There is order in the universe, and it has a uniqueness about it. Cups of coffee always cool off; never do they suddenly get hotter. Things tend to fall apart; never do they suddenly reconnect or reassemble. Order is something we just take for granted—that is, unless we start to lose it. Only when we have to change do we realize how difficult it is to do things differently. Change is an essential part of today's management, but it is one that few leaders or organizations truly understand.

More and more we feel a sense of chaos, an utter sense of confusion about how to do something or even what to do. But there is help, and it comes from an unlikely source. The term *chaos* has another meaning and comes from the field of mathematics. Here we can begin to understand how the real world operates, what makes it tick, and how we can best adapt to the new realities of constant and unexpected change. The mathematic term *chaos* refers to discovery that much of the world operates in a nonlinear mode. In this world, as with our minds, one plus one does not always equal two. Rather small events or actions can have big and often unpredictable and uncontrollable consequences.

Chaos theory has wide application far beyond the field of mathematics, physics, chemistry, biology, or the other pure sciences. It, along with the so-called science of complexity, will revolutionize organizations and the way we lead them because it gives us a deeper understanding of how all things work. It can also be used to build a foundation for understanding creativity.

There is a theory that creativity arises when individuals are out of sync with their environment. Nobel physicist Murray-Gell Mann, in discussing learning, noted that something must have sufficient regularity (order) for it to be able to exploit learning or adapting, but not so much regularity that nothing happens (Mann 1994, 116). This leaves out a large number of things in the universe, including many organizations and some people.

Creative thinking, as we saw in chapter 1, comes in part from asking insightful questions. It comes from challenging your basic assumptions and then redefining ourselves. All this requires that we use broad guidelines for thinking and solving problems rather than a detailed set of standard operating procedures (SOP). Yale economist John Geanakoplos and Minnesota professor Larry Gray demonstrate this type of thinking by explaining about chess-playing computer programs. Grandmasters and some of the more advanced expert system chess players use *rules of thumb* rather than comprehensive analysis to win. These rules can be adapted and used by organizations and individuals to facilitate creative thinking. The key is that there is some order here but not too much. Likewise, some flexibility is allowed, but not so much that thinking becomes chaotic and unpredictable. These rules are the following:

- Favor moves that increase options
- Shy away from moves that end well but require cutting off choices
- Work from strong positions that have adjoining strong positions
- Balance looking ahead to really paying attention to what is happening now on the whole board (Kelly 1994, 426)

These rules of thumb start with reality. This is knowledge we can use as we begin to think about approaching problems in an innovative way. It is a way to remove the bureaucracy and when we do that, we encourage innovative approaches.

## SELF-ORGANIZED CREATIVITY

We all create patterns of behavior whenever we interact with our environment. These patterns are said to have a *self-organized criticality nature.* The analogy of a sand dune has often been used to describe this unique pattern. Per Bak, a Danish-born physicist, came up with this vivid metaphor to explain the concept. He said to imagine a pile of sand on a tabletop, with a steady drizzle of new sand grains raining down from above. The pile grows higher and higher until it can't grow any more.

Old sand then cascades down the sides and off the edges of the table as fast as the new sand dribbles down. The resulting sandpile is self-organized in the sense that it reaches a steady state all by itself, without anyone explicitly shaping it. The sandpile is in a state of criticality because the sand grains on the surface are just barely stable. This is where the originality, the unexpected, the creative part occurs.

When a falling grain hits, there is no telling what will happen—maybe nothing, maybe a tiny landslide or even a catastrophic one. Big avalanches are rare and small ones are frequent, but the steady flow of sand grains triggers all sizes. They follow mathematics called *power or scaling laws,* by which the average frequency and size of a given size of avalanche is inversely proportional to some power of its size. There are a few large ones and many more small ones, but all sizes of avalanches are represented. A well-known power or scaling law measures the energy releases in earthquakes and was discovered long ago by Charles Richter (Mann 1994, 98–99).

Researchers at IBM's Thomas Watson Research Center brought Per Bak's sandpiles metaphor into reality when they built an artificial sandpile to study this behavior. In one experiment, they dropped 35,000 grains of sand onto the pile one by one. As the slope of the sand grew too steep, avalanches would occur. The size of these avalanches demonstrated what is called chaos theory because the outcome of dropping any single grain of sand could not be predicted, but the pattern of the avalanches illustrated part of a phenomenon called self-organized criticality. Grains organized themselves to slope at a certain angle. It was a precarious angle on the edge of chaos because a tiny bit of sand could knock the whole thing down (Lemonick 1993). Like the creative mind, it was not quite stable and not quite chaotic but it was self-organized.

Biophysicist Stuart Kauffman notes that the same self-organized criticality exists in biological evolution and believes evolution proceeds between order and chaos (Waldrop 1992, 304–308). So what does this have to do with creativity? If there is too much order, we become frozen and cannot change. If there is too much chaos, the system retains no memory of what went on before. Their observations are just as relevant to the subject of creativity as they are to sand piles and biology. Chaos, messy confusion, and making new connections are essential to creativity and innovative thinking. As noted in chapter 1, our brains are also nonlinear so a small input, like a grain of information, can produce disproportional changes in the way we think and the connections we are able to make.

## A STATE OF REASONABLE DISORDER IS ESSENTIAL TO CREATIVITY

Spontaneous self-organization has relevance to you and me because it means that *self-organization* can and does occur and not just to sandpiles and biological organisms. People trying to satisfy their day-to-day needs unconsciously organize themselves into an economy through a wide range of individual acts of buying and selling. Anyone hoping to encourage a creative work climate must understand and believe that such systems do not need to be overcontrolled; they will self-organize. We do not need reams and reams of bureaucracy. It will give us order, but in the tradeoff we will lose our originality. Order is something that will emerge; it does not have to be overplanned. Patterns and control emerge without anyone being in charge or consciously planning it. Excessive rules simply destroy the innovative atmosphere by creating a frozen, rigid atmosphere by which procedures are more important than people. How we do something becomes more important than why!

For a person or a business to be in a state of equilibrium (no change) between order and chaos would require that this state be closed to the exchange of matter or energy within its environment. Being in such a state of equilibrium is not a nice place, in fact it is a very dangerous place. Achieving such a balance between order and chaos might sound like a good idea, but it is not. The second law of thermodynamics emphasizes that any equilibrium system that begins to have a measure of disorder called entropy will inevitably increase. Things do not stay the same. Murray-Gell Mann recounts an old physics joke, which says that the first law of thermodynamics says you can't win, but the second law says you can't even break even. The first law of thermodynamics states that the conservation of energy or total energy in a system stays the same, whereas the second law requires the increase in entropy in closed systems. An illustration of this point can be seen in sorting pennies according to dates or nails to size. If someone knocks them over, the odds are overwhelming that the pennies or nails will become all mixed up or disordered. When you make a peanut butter and jelly sandwich, the jar of jelly will likely acquire some of the peanut butter and vice versa. Another example involves two chambers, one containing oxygen, the other nitrogen. When the partition is removed, almost certainly the two will get all mixed up. These examples demonstrate the second law of thermodynamics. Anyone who tries to maintain order in their day or even at their desk understand this basic principle.

## ORDER vs. CREATIVITY

According to the second law of thermodynamics, there are far more ways for nails, pennies, peanut butter, and oxygen to get mixed up than to remain segregated. The second law even gives us an excuse for having a sloppy desk. Now you know why— it's not your fault; it is simply how the universe operates. To the extent that chance is operating, it is likely that closed systems with some order will move toward disorder (Mann 1994, 218–220). A dark blue ink droplet that initially forms a sphere in a static bowl of water (equilibrium system) will eventually diffuse to a uniform light blue. It is no longer a single droplet. This second law challenges our common sense because we often assume equilibrium is in perfect balance. The truth is that order, in equilibrium systems, tends to disappear.

The second law of thermodynamics states that entropy occurs in isolated, closed, or equilibrium systems. Closed systems produce continual disintegration of randomness, whereas **open systems,** like our minds, groups, or organizations, overcome entropy by constantly interacting with its environment. This constant interaction is essential to creativity. To do otherwise is sure death. Executives, organizations, and other open, self-organizing systems, unlike closed systems, make use of messy disorder to create chances for growth and creativity (Stumpf 1995).

Normally, when you, your group, or your organization acquire information, it is incorporated. When the new information or some change is perceived as threatening, there is effort to try to accommodate the information by making small changes that are consistent with the past. We try not to think differently; we try to maintain our old ways, the status quo. It is natural for us to seek order and control and to avoid chaos. Such an approach, however, keeps us and our groups from reaching their creative potential.

Closed systems do not allow anything in and eventually experience decay and entropy. Open systems, like our minds and our groups, constantly take in information. This also means that exact control over such a system is impossible. Rigid control enhances order but removes our creative ability to respond to our environment. We and our groups are open systems and, as such, must be able to respond to our environment and not to artificial controls (for example, bosses, rules, regulations, past rituals, and so on). Excessive control and order prevents us from performing creatively and responding in an innovative way. Granted, some control may be essential to maintain reasonable order, but all too often we either overcontrol, micromanage, or remain with the status quo so much that we lose our creativity. Change is a physical, biological, and mental essential. The enemy of creativity is too much order; the friend is reasonable confusion, disorder, and mistakes.

## SHOULD YOU CHANGE?

An example of having too much change and chaos can be seen in the early 1980s when Apple Computer released Apple III and Lisa. Both were failures in the marketplace, not so much because of the concept but rather how it was executed. The earlier success of Apple II meant that the company had plenty of cash flow. Management was still largely in the hands of the founding team, which had little financial or bureaucratic discipline. Apple was in a constant state of confusion with many different R and D projects going on simultaneously (Nonoka and Kenney 1995). Apple was not unique; many companies can slip toward a chaotic system in such a high-velocity environment, created by venture capital and a continual flow of entrepreneurs. Change should not be so overwhelming as to overload one's capacity to adapt. Likewise if so little change occurs then the organization can become essentially a closed system, a stagnant bureaucracy of rigid order. In such systems creativity and new information is neither sought nor desired.

If you work in an extremely stable environment, there is little reason to innovate or develop creativity. There is very little need to change as long as other competitors, customer needs and desires, or your costs do not change. The bad news is that obviously this type of stability, rather than change, is the exception not the rule. It is easy to assume the world is stable, especially when you spend all your time following those never-changing bureaucratic rules. Why wouldn't you assume that everything remains pretty much the same? It is a dangerous game to assume things are the way they always will be. The biggest risk for many is not recognizing a subtle but changing environment. The chances of recovery, when this occurs or when you get blind-sided, are very slim. When a new competitor, like Japan, acts in a predatory fashion and moves into the environment of automobile manufacturing, it spells long-term trouble for those who still assume they are in a stable environment. Automobile manufacturing, despite what many executives had assumed, is also subject to rapid changes. How do you avoid being blind-sided by change?

# ENVIRONMENTAL SENSITIVITY

Environmental sensitivity is essential to successful innovation. A perfect example of that was Xerox's Alto, which was created in-house in 1973. Their computer system had the advantage of several firsts. It had the first graphics-oriented monitor, the first handheld mouse, the first word-processing program for nonexpert users, the first object-oriented program language and the first laser printer (O'Brien and Smith 1995). It should have been a winner—but it wasn't. So what happened?

Xerox, at the time, only went for the large, expensive technological marketing plans. Finding out about this new Alto market would cost $10 million and Xerox chose not to spend this relatively small amount. The company never consulted potential customers; it kept all development secret and so managed to get *no* feedback and no understanding of what the customer wanted. The result was a failure and no profit.

Successful innovation requires ways of assessing where one is relative to your competition. The following questions need to be answered:

- How do my products and process technologies compare with those of others?
- Are new ideas appearing in my competitors' products sooner than mine?
- Are my new products and processes timely?
- Are projects going according to plans and expectations?
- Is my product and process development cycle time shorter than that of others?
- Are my products accepted by consumers and recognized as high-quality, high-value products when first introduced? (Howard and Guile 1991)

Deciding what innovations to pursue is a big issue. We need to be open to innovation and seek applications and explore options, but ultimately it becomes a matter of where and how much effort to invest in various products and services. Which ideas will be easier to make, sell, or service? Do we invest in known technology or ones that could potentially leapfrog the competition? Ultimately, organizations will choose to pursue those innovations that best match the company's current and expected operational capabilities. This is, however, no assurance of success. The future and subtle shifts in cost, competitive and consumer demands make accurate prediction impossible. Perhaps the best advice can be summarized as follows:

- Use as many tools as possible to continually read your environment—be sensitive to small changes.

- Have a clear direction or purpose for the organization (for example, customer service, profits, quality, and so on) and continually keep people focused on that horizon.
- Invest in as much R and D as practically possible.
- Cultivate a diverse culture and continually encourage horizontal communication and exposure to each other's ideas.
- Hire people with diverse knowledge and interest in many areas, then allow them the opportunity to seek novel solutions (for example, limit bureaucracy, red tape, approvals, regulation SOPs, and so on).

Creativity and innovativeness require great sensitivity to your environment. That is why it is important to know something about the changes occurring around you. Chapter 9 more fully explores how to manage without micromanaging. Filling out the Innovative IQ Questionnaire in chapter 14 (see Exercise #5) is also a good start for those who want a more creative workplace. Creative characteristics like those in the questionnaire give you an ability to change directions, think in new ways, and respond in a flexible manner. Rigid rules, regulations, routines, strict lines of authority, rigid divisions, functions, and departments' responsibilities may help to maintain order, predictability, and even give one a sense of community or culture, but it can impair your ability to respond in creative new ways.

# SUMMARY

When Gottlieb Daimler and Ramson Olds invented an improvement on the horse, they did not know automobiles would fill the countryside (Steward 1993). When the automobile did come, not only did the horse and buggy become extinct but so too did the smithy, harness maker, and a variety of other related niches. This single change in turn created thousands of innovations in jobs, affecting such jobs as building houses, making lawnmowers, and delivering pizza. The automobile also brought forth entirely new innovations like gasoline stations, motels, shopping malls, and even fast-food restaurants. Then as now, when one change occurs, other changes both obvious and subtle will come and go.

S. J. Gould in *Bully for Brontosaurus* tells us that extinctions are also a regular occurrence on earth. Researchers suggest that they occur almost on a regular basis or about every 26 million years or so. The most famous of these was the mass extinction of the dinosaurs 65 million years ago. However, the greatest mass extinction occurred about 225 million years ago when 95 percent of all species on earth disappeared. The serial killer was thought to be rapid *change* in the environment and the close relationships and partnerships that had been built up among the species. Today, we remain no less interdependent. Each niche in nature and in business is affected by and affects others in a continual coevolutionary dance. If the tiny ocean plankton were to be destroyed somehow, oxygen on the planet would drop and even organisms not living in oceans, including humans, would become extinct.

Business interactions may be far more subtle but nevertheless just as interconnected as the natural world. The ability to create strategic plans that prevent such
extinctions or actually produce more fit organizations is extremely limited. Evolution and a field known as chaos theory show us that there is always a great deal of
randomness in nature. It seems that to survive we need to be competitive, adaptive,
and lucky! In nature and business, part of this luck is to be in the right place at the
right time, which demands creativity and a continual process of innovation.

Global competition can both create and destroy a wide range of niches. Therefore, it pays to closely monitor your whole competitive landscape including those
categories G through L in the Innovative IQ Survey (see Exercise #5 in chapter 14).
People speak of global societies. What that means to you and me is that government deficits and interest rates can change stock values and throw your business
completely out of whack. That is why we must continue to create and innovate. If
your Creativity Index (A–F) is low and your environment is in greater flux (G–L),
then you are truly at risk of going the same way as the horse and buggy.

A key concept for remaining a competitive person or group is to create a nonequilibrium process that operates between random chaos and rigid order. Everyone
understands that you can have too much chaos, but you can also have too much
order, stability, and control. This applies to all facets of life. For instance, two Harvard researchers report—much to their surprise—that heart attack patients at highest risk are those with unusually regular patterns of cardiac activity. Healthy hearts
are more irregular, more chaotic (Ferchat 1990). The trick, it seems, in life is to stay
in the zone between the edge of static equilibrium and the edge of chaos. It is this
middle that defines the creativity zone. Next, we will look at how to get in this zone.

# REFERENCES

Ferchat, Robert A. 1990. The chaos factor. *Corporate Board* 11, no. 62 (May–June): 8.

Howard, W. G., and B. Guile. 1991. Profiting from innovation: Management tools
and techniques, part I. *Manufacturing Review* 4, no. 4: 237–45.

Kelly, Kevin. 1994. *Out of control.* Addison-Wesley Publishing Company.

Lemonick, Michael D. 1993. Life, the universe and everything. *Time,* 22 February,
63–64.

Mann, Murray-Gell. 1994. *The quark and the jaguar.* New York: W. H. Freeman and
Company.

Nonoka, Ikujiro, and Martin Kenney. 1995. Towards a new theory of innovation
management. *IEEE Engineering Management Review* 23, no. 2: 6.

O'Brien, C., and S. J. E. Smith. 1995. Strategies for encouraging and managing technological innovation. *International Journal of Production Economics* 41, no. 1–3
(October): 303–18.

Stumpf, Stephen A. 1995. Applying new science theories in leadership development activities. *Journal of Management Development* 14, no. 5 (May): 42.

Waldrop, M. Mitchell. 1992. *Complexity: The emerging science at the edge of order and
chaos.* New York: Simon & Schuster.

# CHAPTER 3

# Thinking Creatively

## INTRODUCTION

Embracing new ideas, new procedures, and new information is essential to innovative thinking. This chapter discusses how to foster creativity by sharing knowledge and information. This includes the need for having a diverse staff with dissimilar viewpoints. An example includes 3M's Technical Forum, a creative culture that promotes the exchange of ideas. Several techniques are examined including the following:

- Rejuvenation
- Cross-fertilization
- Opposite thinking
- How to look for unreasonable solutions

An exercise at the end of the chapter titled *Thinking Outside the Box* will help you and others begin to think in different ways.

So how do you get yourself, your group, your department, or your organization into the creative zone? How do you to find creative solutions to today's problems? It begins with a simple idea. Michael Eisner, CEO of Disney, believes that *synergy* can be the single most important contributor to profit and growth in a creatively driven company. His concept for synergy does not refer to the results of two companies merging. Rather, for him, it means that, when you embrace a new idea, a new business, or a new product, you must make sure everyone in the company knows about it. It is also important that every segment of the business know about it early enough so it can be promoted or its potential exploited in every other possible market, product, or context (Eisner 1996, 10).

William E. Coyne, Senior Vice President of Research and Development at 3M, also understands the imperative of having open and extensive communication. He believes that it is essential for management to communicate with their labs and vice versa, as well as innovators communicating with each other. This way of leveraging their discoveries allows companies the opportunity to get the maximum return on their investments (Coyne 1996).

Most businesses are aware that a natural synergy exists in the normal product cycle. If a product does well domestically, it almost ensures later success in international distribution. Disney makes a point to focus on additional uses of the creative product. The outcome is often an entirely new business for them. For instance, stage musicals are often drawn from successful movies. Synergy is made fun of by many, but at Disney the concept is alive and well.

## BUILDING SYNERGY—THE NEED FOR NONSENSE

*Different thinking* is the very definition of creativity and is an essential part of organizations like Microsoft. Bill Gates believes that business can expect that a crisis will occur every three or four years. He says you have to listen carefully to all of your smart people. That is why Microsoft tries to attract a lot of people who think in different ways (Schlender 1998).

Studies on creativity do, in fact, support Gates's emphasis on the need for different-thinking people. Such people are needed to help us challenge our common sense. Creativity demands that we accept nonsense, not common sense, as our guiding principle. These studies reveal that the diversity in team members' backgrounds, as well as a mutual openness to ideas, can enhance creativity (Albrecht and Hall 1991). A good example of how this diversity can aid creativity can be seen with Canon's 35mm camera.

Canon was founded in 1933 with the purpose of developing a 35mm camera. The company grew rapidly after World War II and throughout the 1950s. By the 1960s it became evident that they would need to diversify into office machinery. A reorganization of Canon in the early 1970s helped them have an annual growth rate of over 20 percent from 1975 to 1985. Canon's success, in large part, can be tracked to the diversity of knowledge they bring to a product development project. They have a large and *diverse* technical staff of more than 3,000 engineers including mechanical engineers (30 percent), electronic engineers (30 percent), physicists (17 percent), chemists (10 percent), and computer-related and other fields (13 percent). Such diverse perspectives provided the necessary creative synergy. To further accelerate diversity, Canon made it a policy to hire mid-career personnel from other firms to create *counterculture* diversity within Canon (Nonoka and Kenney 1995).

The same diversity of knowledge also led to emergence of new ideas for the Apple Macintosh. The Mac team included trained engineers, manufacturing managers, self-taught hackers, and even industrial artists. At one of their meetings a nontechnical person on the team remarked, "how much fun it would be if the Macintosh could sound four distinct voices at once so the user could program it to play music." (Now wouldn't that have sounded like nonsense to most of us?) This prompted a hardware engineer and software programmer to spend hours designing a sound generator with four voices. Diversity of thought was assured because marketing staff, finance specialists, and even secretaries often joined in impromptu discussions (Nonoka and Kenney 1995). It was what one member called group mania that tried to expand what was possible. Team members would create new problems, which caused other members to try to solve them.

Another company that has not only managed to avoid perishing, but rather has figured out how to prosper using synergy, has been 3M. Employees have developed more than 60,000 innovative products since the company was founded in 1902. In 1996 alone they introduced 500 new products (O'Reilly 1997). Their ability to innovate is due in part to an organizational structure in which divisions and departments are given a great deal of freedom to pursue their own projects. Employees spend about 15 percent of their time on their own projects. It is this diversity of ideas that is essential to 3M's business plan (Coyne 1996).

3M's management understands the importance of sharing information. They build synergy among employees by conducting corporate-wide trade shows to expose their employees to new information and innovation in other departments. One example of such programs is the 3M Technical Forum, which was created in 1951 to encourage free and active interchange of information. These technical forums and fairs are organized and managed by the technical people. They also conduct technical audits to help networking and transfer of technology from one 3M business to another. Management also emphasizes that networking is everyone's responsibility. If someone from another lab calls, employees are encouraged to use their 15 percent self-managed time to help them out. This cross-fertilization of ideas has led to dynamic solutions.

Post-it® Notes are perhaps their most famous example of synergy. In 1972, Spencer Silver was trying to create a super strong adhesive; instead he created a super weak one. It was a real setback, so he consulted his colleagues in gluing to see if they knew of a use for it. The whole thing seemed so hopeless. No one could think of a use for a glue that did not stick very well. You can almost hear some boss saying that it was nonsense—it all seemed contrary to the whole point. It all might have ended there, except for another engineer named Art Fry, who had been dealing with his own problem.

## EXPOSE PROBLEMS TO OTHER PERSPECTIVES

Fry had been using slips of paper for bookmarks, which kept falling out, so he applied Silver's *useless* glue to the paper. The bookmarks stuck but didn't tear the page when they were removed. When he tried to convince their marketing people that the invention was useful, they said, "Who would buy an adhesive bookmark? Slips of paper work just fine." But Fry did not give up. Over the next five years he passed out samples of sticky bits of paper to secretaries (who obviously saw the product from a different perspective than engineers). Secretaries not only found a use for them, they became addicted to them. Fry's persistence and the exposure to a broader perspective (secretaries) eventually led to the product called Post-it® Notes. Today the product is one of the five most popular products of the $15 billion company.

# A PERSPECTIVE ON CREATIVITY

It was no accident that secretaries played a key role in the awareness of the potential for Post-it® Notes. An idea's exposure to a *wider perspective* is essential to creativity. Stephen Jay Gould suggests that if genius has any common denominator it would be the breadth of interest and ability to construct fruitful analogies between fields. As an example, Gould, as a scientist, notes that biology's theory of natural selection can be viewed as an extended analogy that Charles Darwin either consciously or unconsciously made to a book he read. That book was Adam Smith's discussion about laissez-faire economics. Smith essentially said that if you want an ordered economy that provides maximum benefits for people, then let individuals compete and struggle for their own advantages. Economic order comes from eliminating and sorting out inefficiencies. Smith emphasizes that economies work best from the struggle among individuals, not from some higher government or other control (Gould 1980).

Gould believes that Darwin's theory of natural selection is an intellectual transfer of Adam Smith's argument for a rational economy to biology. Many would argue about the value of Smith's rational economy, but far fewer experts in the field dispute Darwin's evolution. It is not unusual for an analogy to have a more powerful use in a field other than the original one. This is the likely case when Darwin, having read Smith's work, made the connection that biological order, like economic order, does not arise from higher external control. His realization was that biological order, as well as Smith's economic order, did not occur from the existence of laws operating on the whole but rather came from the struggle among individuals for their own selfish benefits (Gould 1980).

This case clearly demonstrates how creative people can gain insights from other disciplines and knowledges. Darwin's insight into the interworkings of biology was gained, in part, from inductive reasoning about economics and proved more true than Adam Smith's system. Many believe that Smith's rational economy leads to oligopoly and revolution rather than order and harmony. Darwin's analogy led to a revolution in our understanding of our and nature's biology.

# CROSS-FERTILIZATION

How do we get people to begin to explore new ways? To begin with, we have to create a culture, like Disney's and 3M's, that promotes the exchange of ideas and services. This is the opposite of some cultures that emphasize that knowledge is power and refuse to share it. Such attitudes are a prescription for stagnation. Encouraging the exchange of ideas is essential to creativity. Companies like Raychem, Disney, and Fujitsu fight the *knowledge is power* culture through a variety of means. Raychem promotes the stealing of ideas. They recognize that people often suffer from a not invented here syndrome. Many assume if we didn't invent it, it's not very valuable. So Raychem gives an award for adopting others' ideas from within the organization. The trophy and certificate say "I stole somebody else's idea and I am using it." The originator of the idea gets a certificate that says, "I had a great idea and 'so and so' is using it" (Gupta and Singhal 1993). The success of such a system depends upon making sure that both the originator and user of the idea are equally rewarded in terms of promotions and money.

Exchanging ideas is only one way to enhance innovativeness. Sometimes it can be aided by simply changing perspectives. Disney's Michael Eisner believes that a key to creativity, growth, and survival is something he calls *rejuvenation.* They do it by moving their brightest executives frequently to new responsibilities, new businesses, and new contexts. A few years back, their late president, Frank Wells, and Eisner looked around and decided it was seven-year itch time at Disney. The term did not refer to their personal lives, rather it was concerned with continued growth of the company. They believed that a creatively driven company has to constantly renew itself or its ideas dry up and its competitive edge disappears (Eisner 1996, 11).

Disney's answer was to start moving their most promising executives around, exposing them to other parts of the business, increasing their responsibilities, and bringing new eyes and new ideas to their new operations. Then it is top management's job to make sure that their employees are excited about their work and are constantly being renewed. Eisner quoted an old proverb that says, "If you are planning for one year, plant rice. If you are planning for 10 years, plant trees. If you are planning for 100 years, plant people." He then added—plant them, but don't forget to move them around every seven to ten years. New eyes give rise to new ideas and opportunities.

This cross-fertilization is also used by Japanese manufacturers Fujitsu and Toyota to develop multiple competence technology—by collaborating in automotive electronics. These and other Japanese manufacturers innovate by using interlinking experiences from different areas and different disciplines. A strong technological intelligence, overlapping technical development, horizontal information flow, and a continuous search for ideas and refinement are keys to their success (O'Brien and Smith 1995).

The philosophy of Fujitsu's management dovetails with the concept of cross-fertilization. It is similar to the goal of an aspiring small start-up company that wants to maintain an entrepreneurial spirit. The company tries to deemphasize bureaucracy and to avoid doing something because "that's the way it's always been done." Such *why thinking* is encouraged by setting up profit centers for all its product divisions and subsidiaries. Even their research and development (R-and-D) division is expected to act as a profit center.

Only about 50,000 of Fujitsu's total 130,000 employees work for the parent company, with the rest employed in its subsidiaries. Their approach toward their subsidiaries creates the opportunity for divergent thinking to thrive. The parent company believes each subsidiary has its own personality and is given wide operational latitude. The objective is to stay at arm's length from its subsidiaries and not encourage them to look to headquarters for answers. Senior leadership believes that there is no reason for them to interfere as long as a manager is successful.

Managing their R-and-D centers in Richardson, Texas and Middlesex, England, in this manner helps the parent company take advantage of the divergent viewpoints that cross-cultural exchange creates. It also provides advantages for customers because they can have access to locally designed and engineered products. They recognize that different marketplace environments require different degrees of order versus creativity.

## WORK IN AREAS UNRELATED TO YOUR OWN

Fujitsu's philosophy of cross-fertilization allows employees to work in areas not directly related to their immediate area. The company believes this approach enhances the potential for innovation and reduces rivalry within the company. An example of their approach involved a wholly owned subsidiary called Fujitsu Laboratories. This laboratory uses a "one-third rule," which means that one-third of the total work performed is based on contracts from headquarters. Another one-third of their budget allocation is reserved to a particular product the lab is working on, and the last one-third is reserved for pure or basic research. This is similar to 3M's 15 percent rule. The purpose of the one-third rule is to encourage the lab to keep attracting contract business and interact with other groups (Denton 1993, 1–3).

# THINKING OPPOSITE

Certainly one cornerstone of creativity rests on perfecting our ability to think in opposite or reverse ways. The Sony Walkman provides a classic example of opposite thinking. Who would have even imagined people wanting a miniature tape recorder that didn't record? (Haskett 1993) Surely that would have been considered pure nonsense.

No one better demonstrates opposite or different thinking than author and millionaire Warren Buffett. He says that rather than looking for new businesses with new technologies, he does the opposite. He looks for businesses in which he can predict what they are going to look like in 10 or 15 or 20 years. This means that businesses will look more or less like they do today, except that they will be larger and doing more business internationally. So he focuses on an absence of change! If he sees an industry or company that can be hurt by change, he avoids it (Schlender 1998).

Steve Wynn, CEO of Mirage Resorts, also put this opposite-thinking approach into practice. His resort, the $475 million Treasure Island casino hotel, is the first one in Las Vegas designed to generate more revenue from nongambling sources than from gambling! Think of that—build a casino in Las Vegas and focus on great service, great food, and entertainment—what a novel idea. Mirage's soaring stock price has averaged 22 percent a year for the past decade. This opportunity from opposite thinking has also resulted in a hotel with a 99.4 percent occupancy rate and a $1.35 billion casino under construction (O'Reilly 1997, 62).

Another good example of ingrained opposite thinking is that of Southwest Airlines. They have the most productive workforce in the U.S. airline industry. An annual average of 2,400 customers served per employee is twice the number served per employee of any other airline. They also get more daily departures per gate and more productive hours out of an airplane than anyone else in the industry. They also have the lowest turnover rate in the airline industry (Freiberg and Freiberg 1996, 7). The company has been number one in customer service for many years by challenging basic assumptions. When other airlines were creating big hubs in major cities and flying out from them like spokes on a wheel, Southwest used point to point. They made no connections at a central hub; rather they fly between one city (for example, Dallas) to another (Austin) to another (Houston) to another (Dallas). They do not serve meals but instead give their customers peanuts. Flight attendants do not wear uniforms; they wear polo shirts and shorts. Their CEO practices opposite thinking when he says, "If we think small, we'll grow big, but if we think big, we'll grow small" (Freiberg and Freiberg 1996, 78).

Edwin Land and a handful of people thought differently and in the process created the first Polaroid camera in the mid-1940s. They also created one of the world's most innovative companies. Sometimes creativity comes from a flash of insight, at other times it comes from developing a habit of thinking differently. Polaroid's story is the story of instant photography. Land was taking pictures of his little daughter, Jennifer, and after a while she looked up at him and said, "Daddy, why can't I see the pictures right away?" This was the beginning of an idea that led Land to create the whole instant photographic system in a matter of a couple of days (Buckler and Zier 1996).

Land was a creative genius but he also had another admirable quality. He helped to teach others how to be more creative by thinking outside the box. He did that by teaching them to **look for unreasonable solutions.** One employee tells how Land's thinking saved the day. One Polaroid employee explained how he used this knowledge to solve one of his problems. A few years before he had been cutting wood in the fall. He noticed he had his favorite pair of reading glasses in his shirt pocket. At that moment, he looked down and thought he'd better put them in the house. Then he thought he would be careful and not lose them—but he did. As dusk approached, he realized that they were gone. The glasses had brown rims and the woods were full of brown leaves. He spent about 20 minutes looking for the glasses but could not find them.

It was starting to get dark when he dejectedly trudged back slowly into the house. He was thinking that he'd look for them tomorrow when it was bright and sunny. Then suddenly he stopped and remembered something he had learned at Polaroid. He said that Land had told them, "If the solution that you've been pursuing doesn't work, think of the opposite, try the exact opposite. Even if that doesn't work, then it opens up more space anyway."

## IF WHAT YOU'RE TRYING DOESN'T WORK, DO THE OPPOSITE

Immediately, an idea came to him. He thought, "I don't want to look for those glasses in bright sunlight, I want to look for them when it's pitch black. When it is dark, I'm going to go out there with a lantern and those glasses are shiny and those leaves are dull so black is good, dark is good." He got so excited he could hardly wait for dark and could hardly eat his dinner. Finally, when it was dark he ran outside with the lantern and in about five seconds he saw those glasses shining from a hundred yards away (Buckler and Zier 1996).

Another example of opposite thinking comes from Kevin Kelly in his book *Out of Control*. In it he describes a fiber-optic network connecting Kansas City, San Diego, and Seattle, which requires 3,000 miles of cable. The question is, "How much more cable is required to add Salt Lake City?" The answer is none at all. By adding Salt Lake City as a hub and running lines to the three cities through Salt Lake you only need 2,850 miles or 5 percent less than to link the original three. Normal thinking would have been to eliminate Salt Lake because of the extra cable that would be needed, but in fact it shortens the length. The creed of opposite thinking is *more can be less*.

Kelly goes on to tell of Dietrich Braess, a German operations researcher, who demonstrated that adding routes to a congested network can actually slow it down! This is known as Braess's Paradox. It comes from when city planners in Stuttgart tried to ease downtown congestion by building a new street. Traffic got worse after the new street was opened. Planners decided to block off the street and traffic improved. It is not what you might normally think, but sometimes opposite thinking will get you more for less. Sometimes if you want more control, you really need less.

Sometimes you should hire people when you don't need them and raise money when you've got plenty. Some of this opposite thinking has worked for Thermo Electron.

## A DIFFERENT STRATEGY

Thermo Electron, like Polaroid, has used opposite thinking to gain competitive advantages. The successful multimillion dollar company gives new meaning to the word *diversity*. Among other industries, they create biomedical instruments, mammography equipment, power generation, radiation detection, soil recycling, and de-inking technology.

Thermo Electron's sales of instrumentation accounts for approximately 66 percent of their revenues, and the company is number one in the $12 billion market. The company was founded in 1956 and went public in 1967, and today's annual revenues total more than $3 billion. In 1996, the company was added to S & P 500 Index and both the Fortune 500 and Forbes 500 list. The company now has a total of 21 public subsidiaries and is a worldwide leader in paper-recycling equipment and makes the only implantable heart-assist device approved by the U.S. Food and Drug Administration. They spent $300 million, or 10 percent of revenues, on R and D in 1996, and believe that a 100 plus new venture projects and businesses reside within the company. They got where they are by thinking opposite.

Their hiring demonstrates this opposite thinking. Thermo Electron's approach is, if you find someone who is outstanding, hire him or her even though you don't have a job for him or her. The reasoning is, by the time you need to hire somebody, you may not find the right person. They look for intelligence, drive, and ambition, not necessarily educational background.

George Hatsopoulos, founder and CEO of Thermo Electron, was asked why he did not recruit or hire from Sloan School of Business at MIT or Harvard since they are *in their backyard*. Hatsopoulos first noted that Thermo Electron is not reluctant to hire these graduates, but does admit that the number hired from Harvard and MIT are smaller than a company of their size might hire. He went on to say that they like to hire people who have an open mind and are willing to learn that there are other ways of slicing the pie or solving a problem (Key Executive 1997).

As an example of what he meant, he said, "Suppose we hire someone from Harvard Business School. The graduate will look at our balance sheet and say, 'I don't understand why you have so much cash and you don't have more debt. In fact, most companies should have less cash and more debt.'" Hatsopoulos said these graduates cannot understand why that is the case. They are taught in school that having cash is a bad thing because cash can earn about 4 to 5 percent by putting it in CD or other investment.

Thermo Electron's approach is different. They never raise cash when they need it. They only raise cash when they *don't need it* because they have observed that when you don't need cash, people are more willing to give it to you. When you need cash, it becomes more difficult to get it. When you don't need it, you get cash cheaply. They reason that when you need cash, so too do a lot of other people. If you raise cash when nobody needs it, investors will want to invest in your company. Then you hold onto the cash. The business cycle goes on, you wait a couple of years, and you will find everyone is short of cash! Hatsopoulos says, "We have bought companies during difficult times at half the price they were commanding when the economy was great" (Key Executive 1997). In 1997, they started the year with 1.8 billion in cash and wanted to have over 2 billion in cash. In true opposite thinking, they accumulate cash in order to use it at the most appropriate time, which is when everyone is short of cash. Thermo Electron did not think they would have an opportunity to buy because of the booming economy. However, they found an industry in recession—the paper industry. They felt this was a good opportunity for an acquisition so they bought Black Clawson. According to Hatsopoulos, timing is important, a principle never taught in places like Harvard Business School.

Thermo Electron has been most successful with new projects when its employees first identify new or developing needs and then make a product to fit that need, rather than create a product and then convince the market of its usefulness. Founder and CEO George Hatsopoulos says that their most successful projects do not occur when the idea comes from the technologists in search of a need. These engineers and technologists are fascinated with technology and come up with some very intriguing products and they say "Who could use that?" However, this approach does not work most of the time. Rather the better approach is to discover a need and try to find the technology that can meet it. That requires bringing together a team that first identifies the need and they quickly respond with a product to fill it (Rauch 1997).

An example of this process occurred with the passage of the Clear Air Act of 1970. Their staff foresaw the need to measure oxides of nitrogen in the air and was the first company to begin work on the technology. Being first was a big advantage.

The Thermo Instruments System, as the $1.2 billion division was named, had a one-year jump on the competition. They got wind of the potential need and started working far ahead of the major established instrument companies. Hatsopoulos recalls, "We ended up having a monopoly with a product that could meet that need. It took Beckman, the leading instrument company at the time, two years to come up with their own model. By the time they did come in, we had established a name for ourselves. They became 'me-too's' rather than being the first" (Rauch 1997).

The same *anticipating the need* philosophy occurred when they saw the need for a replacement heart when health experts revealed that heart disease was among the country's leading causes of death. They worked on the new venture for 30 years, but were ahead of their competitors in getting a product to market first. Hatsopoulos says, "That's the trick to having a successful enterprise: perceiving a need even before it makes headlines and working on it to try to find a technological solution" (Rauch 1997). It is an approach that has worked well for them, but it is not the only successful approach. 3M takes quite the opposite—or at least different—approach.

# REVERSE PLANNING

3M values opposite thinking because they think it helps them to find solutions by creating unique perspectives. J. Marc Adams, Vice President of Marketing, says that 3M believes the value of strategic planning has been overstated. Those dedicated to the strategic planning model typically ask the following three questions, in the following order:

1. First, in what industries or businesses do we want to operate?
2. Second, within that industry, in what markets or product lines do we want to compete?
3. And, third, what technologies do we need to acquire to enable that competition?

Adams said that his company has noticed that their most successful and most profitable businesses develop when they ask these questions *in the opposite order*:

1. What kind of unique, proprietary technologies do we have?
2. Next, what unique, proprietary products can we make from these technologies?
3. And, finally, to what industries or businesses and for what applications can we sell these products? (Adams 1997)

3M's approach is different than Thermo Electron's approach, which focuses on being first to discover a need, not on maximizing the use of proprietary technologies. Both, however, are in different markets with different objectives than their competitors. So the main point is to be different than your competitors. For instance, 3M applied their opposite thinking when they looked at the electronics industries five or ten years ago. If they had approached this process in the normal manner, they would have first wanted to know what products they would have wanted to make. They would have looked at their potential customers and tried to figure out their needs based on what they could learn from these customers. If they had decided that the most attractive area, the one with the highest margins and most promise for rapid growth, was semiconductors, then they would have purchased the technology, equipment, and personnel for the business. Others who follow the typical strategic model would have done the same thing.

Instead, 3M used opposite thinking. They looked at their proprietary technologies and recognized that some of them could be used in making flexible circuits. Other proprietary technologies could be used to enhance the brightness and battery life of laptop computers. Still others could be used to polish silicon wafers.

By thinking in opposite ways, they were able to develop unique niches. They were able to sell hundreds of millions of dollars of products and build a multibillion-dollar business by first-not-last-looking at their unique technologies. These products are based on proprietary technology, so they will not face a great deal of competition.

Such opposite thinking is a part of the 3M culture, and it's been going on for a long time. In 1973, 3M manufactured only abrasives. A young researcher named Dick Drew visited an auto body shop to test some new sandpaper. He came into the body shop just as several painters were removing a mask of butcher paper held in place by a very aggressive tape. When the workers were removing the tape, which was the industry standard, they peeled off some of the car's new paint. Drew later noted that they uttered "some of the choicest profanity" he had ever heard (Coyne 1996).

This is where the thinking opposite occurred. Drew was in the abrasive business and might have looked at the ruined paint job as an abrasive opportunity. Generic thinking would be—painters need sandpaper to feather out the chipped paint before applying a touch-up. Instead, he saw that his customers' real problem was the tape they were using. If he could give them a better, less aggressive tape, he would solve their problem. He also realized that two-tone cars were becoming increasingly popular. So he went back to the lab and started work on the world's first masking tape. This was later to become the basis of 3M's tape business.

## THINKING OUTSIDE THE BOX

Warren Buffett knows the importance of diversity in business. He believes it may be even more important than exceptional performance. For instance, he said to suppose that we found a way to clone Jack Welch (CEO of General Electric) and ran off 499 clones of him. Jack continued to run GE and the 499 clones ran the rest of the Fortune 500. He wondered if the Fortune 500 were going to have a higher return on equity five years from now or not?

Buffet does not believe the answer is as simple as it might first appear. He says because if you get 500 Jack Welches out there, they are all doing things in a competitive way that may well produce *lower* returns for American business than if you had a bunch of clods out there and a guy like Welch was competing with them. His point is that if you have got great variation in the quality of management, it

---

**THINKING OUTSIDE THE BOX**

**Procedure**:    Ask the participants to form groups of 6 to 8 people in a circle or around tables. Each person is asked to think about a current job-related problem or concern. Each then writes a simple definition of a problem on a blank sheet of paper. Examples might be "How can I get more customer satisfaction?" or "How can I improve my process?" After allowing a few minutes to think about and write out their problems, ask each person to pass his/her problem to the right. That person reads the problem just received and jots down the first thought that comes to mind in addressing that problem. They are given 30 seconds to respond to that individual sheet. Try not to assume anything and only look for what might eliminate or simplify the problem.

The next person should try to think of something different than has already been suggested. Repeat this process every 30 seconds, and keep the process going until each person gets their original sheet back. Time permitting, they can then discuss some of the more practical solutions offered.

**Discussion
Questions:**

1. Did anyone discover innovative solutions that you had not previously considered?

2. Can you see any value in trying some of these suggestions?

3. Do some of these suggestions help you make connections to other ideas or solutions?

4. What lesson does this show us about different perspectives and viewpoints?

**Materials
Required:**    Paper, notepads, and pencils.

**Approximate
Time Needed:**    10 to 15 minutes.

---

**Figure 3.1.**

improves the chances enormously of a relatively significant number getting terrific returns (Schlender 1998). Buffett, it seems, never has trouble *thinking outside the box.*

Figure 3.1 is a good exercise to help you to begin to think outside your own box. The objective is to obtain several possible innovative solutions or suggestions for your current challenges or problems. Likewise, if you find it difficult to think differently, consider using the checklist for Ways of Finding New Information in Figure 3.2.

---

### WAYS OF FINDING NEW INFORMATION

1. In-house market research
2. Using consultants
3. Collaborative ventures with others
4. Monitoring trade shows
5. Focus groups with customers or employees
6. Suggestion box
7. Problem-solving team
8. Recruiting new staff
9. Monitoring federal R-and-D activities
10. Staff rotation program
11. Moving executives around to other areas
12. Training for creative thinking
13. Storyboarding (see chapter 14)
14. Acquisition of other companies
15. Sabbatical programs
16. Synergy-corporate sharing of ideas
17. Encourage personnel to study outside this discipline

---

**Figure 3.2.**

# SUMMARY

Many might be surprised to discover that many Nobel prizes have been won by scientists outside their main field of expertise (Sebell 1993). Perhaps this is because people who don't know that they cannot do something are open-minded enough to make it possible. What is more surprising perhaps is that this same naiveness also works in business.

Several studies such as Mitchell (1989) and Tushman and Anderson (1986) have revealed that radical innovations tend to be introduced by companies outside an industry or by newcomers rather than by industry incumbents (Gilbert 1994). It seems incumbents are good at doing what they do better, but it often takes the outsider to introduce something that radically alters the way things are done. But often we make little room for them.

In life and in business, there are always tradeoffs, and creativity is no different. Strong cultures and/or strong directive leadership are much prized in part because it can help people stay focused, in control, and organized, but there is a down side. Directiveness and strength of a leader can thwart creativity because it can diminish expressions of divergent views and thinking. Highly cohesive groups can develop group think that produces uniformity of actions but diminishes divergent thinking. It's great when the leader has the good idea, but it's bad when someone else tries to think differently (Nemeth 1997).

In today's organizations it's hard to think differently. Perhaps this is why Xerox has anthropologists, psychologists, and sociologists on their research staff to help them listen in different ways for latent needs and tacit knowledge.

Some organizations are so concerned about keeping some diversity of behavior that they permit employees to buck top management. Marriott says that, "If managers can't explain why they're asking employees to do something, they don't have to do it" (Collins and Porras 1994). DuPont grants employees money to pursue projects turned down by management. Hewlett-Packard instituted a *medal of defiance* presumably based on an employee who defied David Packard and continued to work on a graphics project that eventually turned out to be a big money maker (Nemeth 1997). Motorola and 3M regularly use "venture" teams of people from various disciplines.

# REFERENCES

Adams, J. Marc. 1997. Competing in highly dynamic markets by strategic innovation: The 3M model. *1997 McGill Graduate Business Conference,* 13 February, 25, 26.

Albrecht, Terrance L., and Bradford J. Hall. 1991. Facilitating talk about new ideas. The role of personal relationships in organizational innovation. *Communication Monographs* 58, no. 3 (September): 273–88.

Buckler, Sheldon A., and Karen Anne Zien. 1996. From experience the spirituality of innovation: Learning from stories. *The Journal of Product Innovation Management* 13, no. 1 (March): 403–5.

Collins, J. C., and J. I. Porras. 1994. *Built to last: Successful habits of visionary corporations.* New York: Harper Collins.

Coyne, William E. 1996. Building a tradition of innovation. *UK Innovation Lecture,* 5 May, 5–9.

Denton, D. Keith. 1993. Behind the curve. *Business Horizons* (July/August): 1–3.

Eisner, Michael. 1996. Speech to Chicago Executives Club. Chicago, Ill. 19 April, 10–11.

Freiberg, Kevin, and Jackie Freiberg. 1996. *Nuts! Southwest Airlines' crazy recipe for business and personal success.* Austin, Tex.: Bard Press.

Gilbert, Joseph T. 1994. Choosing an innovation strategy: Theory and practice. *Business Horizons* 37, no. 6 (November/December): 17.

Gould, Stephen Jay. 1980. *The panda's thumb.* New York: W. W. Norton & Company.

Gupta, A. K., and A. Singhal. 1993. Managing human resources for innovation and creativity. *Research Technology Management,* no. 36: 41–48.

Haskett, John. 1993. Creative destruction: The nature and consequences of change through design. *I.D.: Magazine of International Design* 40, no. 5 (September/October): 30.

*Key Executive Interview: Thermo Electron.* 1997. New York: HSBC, James Capel (fall): 28–29.

Mitchell, W. 1989. Whether and when? Probability and timing of incumbents' entry into emerging industry subfields. *Administrative Science Quarterly* 34: 208–30.

Nemeth, C. J. 1986. Differential contributions of majority and minority influence. *Psychological Review* 93: 23–32.

Nemeth, Charlan Jeanne. 1997. Managing innovation: When less is more (creativity in management). *California Management Review* 40, no. 1 (fall): 67–68.

Nonoka, Ikujiro, and Martin Kenney. 1995. Towards a new theory of innovation management. *IEEE Engineering Management Review* 23, no. 2: 4–7.

O'Brien, C., and S. J. E. Smith. 1995. Strategies for encouraging and managing technological innovation. *International Journal of Production Economics* 41, no. 1–3 (October): 303–10.

O'Reilly, Brian. 1997. The secrets of America's most admired corporations. *Fortune* 135, no. 4 (3 March): 60–64.

Rauch, Lisa. 1997. Spinning out and growing. *Entrepreneurial Edge* 2: 25.

Schlender, Brent. 1998. The Bill and Warren show. *Fortune* 138, no. 2 (20 July): 55, 60.

Sebell, Mark H. 1993. What American business must do to remain innovative. *Manage* 45, no. 1 (July): 21.

Tushman, M., and P. Anderson. 1986. Technological discontinuities and organizational environments. *Administrative Science Quarterly* 31: 439–63.

# CHAPTER 4

# Finding New Solutions

## INTRODUCTION

Innovative solutions often come from finding ways to look at old problems in new ways. Entering the creative zone can best be done by thinking more like an artist or scientist than like a bureaucrat. Some ways to do this include the following:

- Paying attention to irrelevant thoughts
- Using analogies and metaphors to make new connections
- Combining and relating divergent disciplines.

Edward de Bono is a management consultant who specializes in thinking concepts. He notes that when it comes to the brain, both information and the surface are active. It is an open system. All information changes the surface, which then receives future information differently. A similar analogy would be rain falling onto a landscape. It eventually gets organized into streams and rivers. These mind patterns are asymmetric, which means our organized thoughts tend to go along main streams or tracks. We do this without ever noticing the side stream (de Bono 1995). The trick is to make the connections so we can get over to this side stream.

Thinking differently, whether it is in reverse or opposite ways or by using metaphors or analogies, does not come naturally. We tend to be like rivers and follow similar paths. We can, however, change course and enter new thought streams. It begins by creating a different consciousness, by creating new connections. Land did this by showing his people how to change their reference point. Darwin did this through exposure to new information including reading material outside his discipline. 3M's Fry gained a new perspective by showing his product to secretaries rather than to engineers or marketing personnel.

There are numerous other ways to gain this different perspective. One of those is used by Francois Castaing, executive vice president of vehicle engineering and general manager of powertrain operations at Chrysler. Castaing reorganized the engineering team, which was grouped into functions such as body, chassis, powertrain, and so on, into vehicle platforms where a design group worked on the total car and not just its components. The first proof that this was a better arrangement was their "Viper," when a team of 75 engineers created the new car in just three years. This was impressive since in the late '80s it normally took about 5 1/2 years to bring a new car to market.

The fear at the time was that the engineers would be so empowered that there might be too much diversity, duplication, or even a lack of sharing. Some worried that there might even be competition among platform teams. So Castaing quickly developed *technical clubs* in which engineers informally agreed to spend an hour over coffee once a week with their counterparts on other platform teams so sharing could be promoted.

Castaing said these tech clubs seemed to help keep complexity and duplication under control. Chrysler suppliers, reduced from over 2,000 to some 300, also helped to enhance communication by relating successes and failures while working with different platform teams. Cross-fertilization among platforms was encouraged to the point that after five years all designers had changed platforms at least once (Stevens 1996). Doing this allowed people the opportunity to experience new perspectives and make connections that normally would not have been made.

## TRANSFER KNOWLEDGE FROM OTHER DISCIPLINES

Creativity does not always come from gaining new perspectives. Developing new connections and insights also requires getting rid of some old prejudices. Business people somehow think that they are different from other professionals. It is okay for the artist or poet to be confused but not a professional. The academic or scientist may walk around in a daze but business people, we are told, are made of sterner stuff. We should just be able to look at a problem logically and deduce the correct solution. Such an approach might work some of the time, and it might get an answer. But will it be a truly creative, inventive, original answer?

To find a truly innovative approach requires thinking in different ways, much like a scientist or even an artist might think. These and other creative types are able to improvise new connections that lead to innovative solutions because they are able to muddle around. The muddling is natural because they are dealing with new information. They are able to think outside the box, to reformulate the problem so they can find new connections. Entering the creative zone means accepting some disorder, confusion, and some messy uncertainty. This healthy state of confusion begins by often paying attention to some irrelevant line of thought.

# VALUE DIVERSITY OF KNOWLEDGE

Edward Steer is the CEO of Pfizer, an American drug company with a reputation for producing innovative and profitable new medicines. He stresses to his researchers that they not fall into the common trap of concentrating on areas in which they are familiar and comfortable. Rather he urges them to stretch into promising new approaches like genetics (O'Reilly 1997). Exploring new areas is a tough process; it is especially difficult if you have too many Xerox copies of each other.

A central principle involved in finding new solutions to production, quality, or service problems is that *diversity of knowledge is essential to creativity.* Some companies have even found it necessary to draw from outsiders to insure this new or different perspective. The Doblin Group is a group of innovation consultants based in Chicago. They send cultural anthropologists to camp out with a client's customers. They watch what their customers do, what they hate or like, and try to come up with new products or services that no one knew they needed. Larry Keeley, Doblin's president, says the marketing department of large companies is often the least receptive to innovation. He says their corporate marketing department often studies data and asks customers what they do not like about their products (O'Reilly 1997). However, because they still carry a narrow viewpoint, they often don't get powerful insights that way.

Some believe that creative ideas emerge deep within the interworking of your mind engine. But just as likely is the possibility that this subconscious or internal working is able to draw in other information sources and make serendipitous connections. An example can illustrate this point. A hospital vice president at a seminar told about a breakthrough she thought she had when she was trying to get the community interested in a new substance abuse program. She said she had tried everything but still was not getting much of a response. It was sometime later, when she was tinkering with her carburetor's gas and air mix, that she suddenly understood what was wrong. She said she had to change the carburetor mix for a different attitude. She then began to advertise the program on TV. The new "mix" or new strategy was a huge success (Harris 1988).

Some would say that her unconscious helped to reach this creative insight, but maybe it was something closer to the surface. If she had not had knowledge of this alien discipline (repair of the carburetor), it is doubtful that the connection would have been made about the problem she was facing. The brain continues to look for solutions—when it faces difficult problems, it seeks input; it seeks new connections. The truth is that we never know when a bit of old, unrelated information will become useful in a new way. It is these different perspectives that give different outcomes.

## BEER AND CHIPS

Analogies can provide an effective link that helps people make connections they might otherwise miss. When Canon was working on a new type of small copier, the feasibility team conducted several camp sessions. These were gatherings of project teams outside the workplace to brainstorm new solutions. The feasibility of these small copiers depended on them being essentially maintenance-free. A new concept that emerged to help do this was *discarding* the entire *drum* after it had made a certain number of copies. A conventional copier drum was a component with an open-ended life but would certainly need repairing. The team conceptualized an entirely new way of thinking about the drum, one with a limited but known life span.

This meant developing disposable photo receptors, development apparatus, and an instant toner-fuser—all within target cost. When the team members said it was impossible to produce the drum inexpensively, the team leader Hiroshi Tanaka drew on an analogy. He purchased some disposable cans of beer and told the team members to drink the beer (and you thought your work was hard). Then he got the members into an argument (wonder how hard that was to do after a few beers) about how much beer cost and what made it so inexpensive. The disposable beer can resembled the copier drum because it would be *disposable*. Making the connection between the drum and the beer can provided the team members with many insights into methods of manufacturing the drum at a lower cost (Nonoka and Kenney 1995).

The story is so odd that it has to be true. Beer cans and copiers, who would even have believed that it would lead to any insight—at least a sober one? But that is the power of analogies and metaphors. They allow us to free up our thinking and make connections that lead to insights that might have been otherwise impossible.

Sony is not the only one to use analogies to create novel insights. At one time, Apple Computer's Macintosh project team conceived of the MAC as a bicycle of personal computers, the telephone of the '80s, the crankless Volkswagen for the quality conscious, and the Cuisinart (Nonoka and Kenney 1995). The idea was to use analogies to help the team create a product become pervasive and impact everyone's life. The goal may never have been totally achieved, but it did help create a unique and distinctive product.

Creativity does not derive from a single cohesive thought, but rather from combinations of unrelated thoughts. *Combining* and *relating* are essential parts of the creativity process in all disciplines (Fiol 1995). Great insights often occur when these streams of thought mix and mingle. This interplay is at the heart of most stories of creativity and innovation.

## FIND DIRECT ANALOGIES* TO YOUR PROBLEMS

Creativity is built on bridging disconnected fields and knowledge. Ioannis Miaoulis, Dean of Tufts University's College of Engineering, is somewhat of an expert at bridging disconnected fields and knowledge. He is helping to solve a problem that has challenged material scientists for years—how to heat microelectronics chips evenly enough during production to avoid melting parts of their very thin film surfaces? His solution came out of combining two quite diverse disciplines—engineering and biology. He believes the tools of engineering can help us to better understand biology, and biological insights, in turn, can lead to better technological designs. His point is that some very difficult technological problems have already been solved by evolution.

*See Figure 4.1 for an explanation of *direct analogies*.

Most people would see little connection between bugs and chips, but Miaoulis is well equipped to make such serendipitous connections. His fluency in areas like economics, optics, and material science is diverse. This diversity of knowledge has often led him to novel solutions. He recalls how he kept hearing of materials-processing researchers complaining about problems caused by heat. It was obvious to him that material processors were not studying the work done by heat-transfer researchers and heat-transfer people were not applying their work to materials processing. The semiconductor business would prove his point.

Computer chips are made in mass from wafers of silicon several inches in diameter and a thin film of silicon oxide, a few hundred-thousandths of an inch thick. The film is then etched to make the detailed circuitry of chips. The final step involves cutting the wafer into 50 or so chips. Before this occurs, chips are heated to extremely high temperatures during some stage of their production. For some reason, never quite understood by materials-processing engineers, the wafers exposed to high temperatures refused to heat evenly. Hot spots develop that get much hotter than the rest of the wafer. They then crack or warp, thereby reducing the number of chips the wafer yields (Smale 1997).

Miaoulis was baffled about the problem as well. The appearance of the hot spots seemed related to the thickness of the film, but in a most bizarre way. Thicker film should, in theory, insulate against hot spots, but in the lab the spots would often get much worse when the film thickness was increased. Miaoulis believed that these hot spots could not be explained by conventional heat transfer. He could not understand what was happening until a couple of years later when he met a student, Paul Zavracky, who was a specialist in optics. Optical physicists study the way light rays are reflected, bent, or absorbed. Light is a wave with alternating peaks and valleys. When light is bounced off a thin film that is half as thick as the light's wavelength, the light ray bounces both off the bottom and the top and is then joined up again, thereby creating a bright light. If the film is three-quarters as thick as a wavelength, its peaks will end up aligning with a top-reflecting wave's valleys and vice versa. The result is that the two waves largely cancel each other out and create weak light.

As Miaoulis listened to Zavracky talk, he thought, "Could the hot spots on chips be an optical effect?" Heat, after all, can radiate light even if it is invisible. Could it be that heat radiating during chip production is reflecting off the top and bottom of the chip's thin-film coating and be creating some spots? Miaoulis later found out that it was indeed the case. He said, "No one had thought about applying optical interference effect to heat," but experiments confirmed the theory. His solution was simple—avoid making thin films the thickness of the wavelength of infrared light. Unfortunately, however, it isn't always practical to avoid making that thickness of film.

Miaoulis began to suspect that there might be a way to produce thin films that were less vulnerable to melting, but he didn't have any idea how to do it. He did, however, have a willingness to look for answers by applying knowledge from diverse areas. While snorkeling, he started staring at a sea anemone. With little locomotive ability, they just sit on the floor and let underwater currents carry plankton to them. He saw this as an interesting engineering problem. An anemone would want to be as wide as possible to catch as much food as possible, but not so large that it is swept away by the current. He reasoned that apparently evolution had engineered the anemone to meet both needs. Miaoulis reasoned that nature had solved a thorny challenge that engineers face every day. It was a straightforward optimization problem of solving two equations simultaneously—one describing stability against the current and the other its volume of food.

Connecting two diverse fields, engineering and evolution, led Miaoulis down a path he still pursues. He later used anemones to test different shapes and found that evolution had indeed found the ideal shape and size for a creature that had to have as much water as possible pass through without being carried away. Reinforced by his success, he started looking at the dynamics of other creatures. He looked at fish, crabs, starfish, mussels, and sea urchins. So what does all of this have to do with mechanical engineering? Miaoulis, in the back of his mind, was hoping that somehow nature's evolution would help to solve problems faced by mechanical engineers. He says, "If you do interesting research, you will find interesting applications." Sometimes it is just a matter of posing the right question. Posing questions is often harder than finding answers (Smale 1997).

## CONNECTING CHIPS AND BUTTERFLIES

It was a couple of years before one of those right questions came to Miaoulis. While sitting in Tufts' cafeteria, he thought, "Did any animal take advantage of the eccentric heat absorption properties of thin films?" He wondered if a creature had evolved with a skin of some sort whose thickness was tuned to reflect the warmth of the sun, while perhaps a close cousin, in a cooler climate with an almost identical skin a mere millionth of an inch thick, was tuned instead to absorb warmth.

Miaoulis thought surely nature must have already hit upon it, but what could this thin-skinned creature be? Thinking about the question, he walked out of the cafeteria and noticed that it was butterfly season. The campus was swarming with them. One alighted on a large rock next to the path where he was standing. It only took a moment to adjust its wings—its brightly hued and really, really *thin* wings.

Today, Miaoulis and his students have an aquarium full of butterflies. They use their lab to roast butterfly wings. Deceased butterflies get the heat treatment on a thin pole that has six electrodes glued to their wings. Butterfly wings, you see, are multilayered thin-film construction with scales on the order of a millionth of an inch thick. So what has come out of roasting a few hundred butterfly wings? It is an observation no biologist would have noticed. Their wings, even under intense heat, always cook evenly. There were no hot spots! (Remember the problem about heating microelectronic chips evenly?)

There are no hot spots despite the fact that butterfly wings are not uniformly thick. In fact, they are rough compared to man-made, thin films. This insight led Miaoulis to challenge traditional thinking. He said we have always assumed that films should be smooth. When we are young we learn flat things work best. A sanded table holds a glass better than one made of rough wood, and you don't get splinters. As a result, engineers have developed a bias for flatness. It is aesthetically pleasing.

Darwin's nature, on the other hand, does not rely on assumptions; it simply tries everything by trial and error, over eons, until it ends up with what works. Miaoulis believes that his butterflies are telling him that rough films may work better than smooth films for manufacturing semiconductor chips. He says he trusts time, and time has rejected flat films for rough ones. At this point, it is unclear why roughness equates to resisting hot spots. Perhaps it has something to do with the effects of random variation serving to break up the potential hot spots. In theory, it should be easier to build rough chips rather than smooth ones, but it may be easier to carve neat designs in smooth ones.

Miaoulis has not yet built any chips with more heat-resistant thin film, but if he does, it will have enormous consequences, including the ability to apply higher temperatures without damaging the chips. His success or failure on this project though is not as significant as his ability to apply diverse knowledge to his field. It has helped him shed old assumptions, frame new questions, and think in opposite and creative ways.

A long history of psychological literature demonstrates that the creative act is the result of multiple viewpoints and broad problem definitions that pull people away from existing solutions (Koestler 1964). Edward de Bono (1968) has called this type of approach lateral thinking.

Thinking differently requires putting yourself in a different frame of reference. One way to do this is to look for connections in metaphorical worlds. For example, in 1959 Allistair Pilkington invented a method for eliminating wavy glass as a result of musing about grease floating on dish water, which, in an open-minded way, led to today's process of manufacturing uniform glass by floating it on molten tin (Gilliam 1993). Analogies compare two things that are essentially dissimilar and serve to encourage creativity because they help you to make connections that otherwise would seem obvious. Analogies and metaphors are also often used to stir up the imagination.

The best advice for using analogies to help you arrive at creative solutions is to do the following:

- Choose a field or area you are familiar with outside of work and apply it to your work situation.
- Create an analogy that allows you the opportunity to use ample facts, knowledge, or technology from this other field to your work problem. Be sure to write out your analogy.
- Write out any insights or potential solutions that the analogy yields.

Figure 4.1, titled *Lateral Thinking Tools,* is designed to help you to think differently by making use of analogies and metaphorical worlds. Try it out, you might find that it opens up a whole world of new possibilities.

Figure 4.1 also provides a brief description of analogies and metaphors. Read this, and then use different knowledge domains like those seen in Figures 4.2 through 4.4 and see if you can come up with a direct analogy. Figures 4.2 and 4.3 are easier because they provide a visual reference. Figure 4.4 is the most difficult because most of us are unfamiliar with these subjects. (Incidentally, Figure 4.4 was

---

### LATERAL THINKING TOOLS

**ANALOGY**
Comparison of things that are essentially dissimilar but are shown through analogy to have some similarity.

- Think of a problem you are having and something else, then ask yourself what insights or potential solutions the analogy suggests.

**METAPHOR**
Figure of speech in which two different thoughts that are linked by some point of similarity (all metaphors) are simple analogies, but not all analogies are metaphors (frozen wages, idea drought).

**SIMILES**
Specific types of metaphors that use the word *like,* or *as* (the wind cuts *like* a knife).

**DIRECT ANALOGIES**
Facts, knowledge, or technology from one field are applied to another field (such as biology to robots—examine spiders and other bugs to improve agility of robots).

- Choose a field of science or area of endeavor that could provide an analogy to your problem.
- Create an analogy that allows you to apply facts, knowledge, or technology from the other field to your problem. Write out the analogy.
- Determine any insights or potential solutions that the analogy yields.

**PERSONAL ANALOGY**
See yourself as personally involved in the problem you are trying to solve—perhaps role play. Can you put yourself into your problem? Then ask yourself what insights or potential solutions the personal involvement yields. (For example, in 1980 Gillette managers pretended to be human hair—and viewed life. I dread being washed everyday, I hate blow-dryers, I feel limp and lifeless—some wanted shampoo to protect damaged ends, others wanted more aggressive ones—everyone had different sentiments. The result was Silkience, a shampoo that adapted itself to different needs and became one of the top 10 shampoos.)

---

Figure 4.1.

**USING VISUAL ANALOGIES #1**

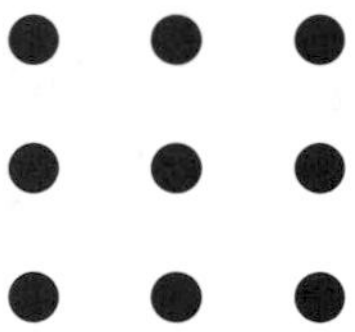

Connect all nine dots by drawing the smallest possible number of straight lines without taking the pencil off the paper. Many assume you have to keep the lines within the square formed by the outer dots, although the constraint is not part of the problem as stated. A crucial step in solving the puzzle would be to find out whether there is any reason to confine the lines inside the square.

QUESTION:    How can you use this analogy to help you determine the boundary of a problem you are facing? Use it to help you reassess the latitude you're giving yourself in solving the problem.

Figure 4.2.

**USING VISUAL ANALOGIES #2**

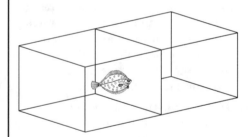

Take a fish and put a pane of glass halfway through the fishbowl. Several days later remove the glass. The fish will stay on its side. It assumes that's all it can do even if no barrier remains.

QUESTION:    Think of a current problem you are having. Describe what you think are the current barriers, then go back to each and challenge why you believe these exist.

Figure 4.3.

**SECOND LAW OF THERMODYNAMICS ANALOGY**

The Second Law of Thermodynamics states that entropy applies in all isolated and closed systems. Entropy, a process of continual disintegration to a state of randomness, is a predictable outcome of any system in the absence of new inputs. Open systems overcome entropy by interacting with the environment—taking in needed resources.

Self-organizing system theory posits that open systems use disorder to create possibilities for growth. Through both resilience and self-reference, self-organizing systems are capable of maintaining an identity while changing form. They have both autonomy and control. Each form that is created works for the moment. If new information supports the form, it persists. If new information threatens the form, the system looks for ways to accommodate the information by making incremental changes that are consistent with much of its past but do not unnecessarily deny the new information or a new future. This *rolling equilibrium* or adjustment is more than a reaction to an action in the Newtonian sense because the reaction is not predictable.

What happens if the autonomy within such systems is removed (that is, if they are externally controlled by the organization)? Self-organizing system theory suggests that in such situations the system will fail to adjust to the environment in a timely manner as it must obtain approval from parts of the organization that have not experienced the environment in the same way. Autonomy is central to the system's evolution. This raises the question, "How does an organization control a self-organizing system?" The answer may be that it does not. The self-organizing system operates within a relatively stable, more global structure. Changes within the local structure tend to have only a minor effect on the global structure. The stability of the global structure stems from its creation over time as a result of the culture, vision, and values shared by the majority of organizational members and key stakeholders.

The leadership development implications of self-organizing system theory are found in the providing of direction and control. First, disequilibrium and disorder are not viewed as negative attributes of such systems. Some degree of each is necessary to provide the system with opportunities to adjust to new information. As adjustments are made, the self-organizing system learns how to accommodate to its environment. Leadership efforts that try to eliminate disorder and control behavior will destroy the system's ability to self-organize. Novelty of response is often necessary. Without new stimuli, which often arises out of discontentedness, people lapse into dull habit. In so doing, the likelihood of maladaptive behavior increases owing to differences in each actor's perceived reality of the situation (Stumpf 1995).

**QUESTION:**    How can this be used to create an organization that is dynamic but stable? (See chapter 9 for some suggestions.)

Figure 4.4.

also the inspiration for chapter 2 and chapter 9 and much of the reasoning about creativity.) If these analogies are too difficult to apply, choose something you are familiar with and write down (1) similarities between your analogy and (2) solutions that usually come from that area and how they might be applied to the problem you are trying to resolve.

# SUMMARY

Thinking in opposite and different directions is an essential component of creativity and innovation. It begins by making yourself open to new perspectives. Many recognize the need to gain new perspectives. Students at Yale University of Medicine under the tutelage of Professor of Dermatology Irwin M. Braverman have been introduced to a method of learning that takes them out of the classroom and into the museum. In a program called the British Museum Project, Dr. Braverman instructs students to observe preselected paintings at the Yale Center for British Art, and make judgments about how thoughts and feelings are communicated visually. His goal is to train students to be more careful observers by extracting more information through observation.

Dr. Braverman believes heightened observation skills help to improve correct diagnosis. He says doctors have to be taught to pick up details that are often overlooked. In metaphorical thinking, he says students are assigned a painting and given time to observe and study it "like a rash that has been framed." Each student describes the work based solely on what he or she sees and learns from group discussions, reactions, and observations. Medical students who participated said it had been a significant step in their medical training (Peart 1998).

Professor Braverman recognizes that the same old knowledge and viewpoint can only produce old solutions. There is ample evidence that the unreflective adoption of premises and old patterns of solving problems is not only detrimental to observation but also to creativity. When we find a solution that works, we tend to use it, even when it no longer is the best one. The power of metaphors and all different thinking tools is that it gets us to think outside the box (Nemeth 1997).

One of the best ways to do creative thinking is to find new ways of making new connections. All such approaches mentioned here require you to expose yourself to new knowledge. Along with diversity of knowledge comes the need to generate as many ideas as possible. A Darwinian approach, which is the subject of chapter 5, insures survival-of-the-fittest ideas. Combining divergent fields, disciplines, and perspectives also encourages lateral thinking. One helpful approach is to identify analogies that have common threads with your current problem.

Finding new solutions requires us to accept nontraditional modes of thinking and new ways of gaining new perspectives. As we have seen in this chapter, many good analogies and different perspectives come from nature and, in particular, evolutionary biology. In chapter 5, we will examine this rich field in greater detail. In the process of understanding should come some new insights on how to develop greater creativity and innovative problem solving.

# REFERENCES

de Bono, Edward. 1968. *New think: The use of lateral thinking in the generation of new ideas.* New York: Basic Books.

———. 1995. Serious creativity. *Journal for Quality and Participation* 18, no. 5 (September): 12.

Fiol, C. Marlene. 1995. Thought worlds colliding: The role of contradiction in corporate innovation processes. *Entrepreneurship: Theory and practice* 19, no. 3 (spring): 71.

Gilliam, Terry K. 1993. Managing the Power of Creativity. *Bank Marketing* 25, no. 12 (December): 15.

Harris, Hollis L. 1988. Recapturing a singleness of purpose. *Air Transport World Conference.* Washington, D.C., 4 October, 13.

Koestler, A. 1964. *The act of creation.* New York: Macmillan.

Nemeth, Charlan Jeanne. 1997. Managing innovation: When less is more (creativity in management). *California Management Review* 40, no. 1 (fall): 64.

Nonoka, Ikujiro, and Martin Kenney. 1995. Towards a new theory of innovation management. *IEEE Engineering Management Review* 23, no. 2: 5.

O'Reilly, Brian. 1997. The secrets of America's most admired corporations. *Fortune* 135, no. 4 (3 March): 60–64.

Peart, Karen. 1998. Yale medical students use artwork to sharpen diagnostic skills. *WWW Eurekalert Org.,* 23 February, 1.

Smale, Brian. 1997. The butterfly solution. *Discover* 18, no. 4 (April): 50–52.

Stevens, Tim. 1996. Converting ideas into profits: Strategic management of the innovation process pays big dividends at the bottom line. *Industry Week* 245, no. 11 (3 June): 48.

Stumpf, Stephen A. 1995. Applying new science theories in leadership development activities. *Journal of Management Development* 14, no. 5: 39–49.

# CHAPTER 5

# Using Darwin's Four Forces to Generate Creative Thinking

## INTRODUCTION

The four forces of evolution will be explained. Natural selection, mutation, genetic drift, and gene flow are how nature works. These four forces can also be used to enhance creativity and spur innovative thinking. Natural selection and mutations indicate the following:

- Create more ideas than you can possibly use
- Acquire new behaviors
- Provide *opportunity* and *motive* for change

Genetic drift shows us why *skunk works* work and why *adversity* is an essential part of developing an atmosphere where innovative thinking can bloom. Adversity comes in many forms including the following:

- Stretch goals
- Setting exceedingly high standards
- Creating *adaptive challenges*

Gene flow, or its counterpart *idea flow,* helps to encourage innovative thinking by encouraging becoming a *you need to know this* organization and by using horizontal learning.

The mechanics of evolution have been with us for a long time, but only recently have they been applied to management. Nature started the evolutionary process with the atom, then the molecule came, and still later came the self-replicating molecules. Finally three billion years later nature evolved intelligence. Today, we know that evolution, in large part, is responsible for all the varieties in humans and other animals. It is not conjecture or even a fact—it is, in fact, a good fact of life. All the differences we see in our species and in other animals are a good thing. Variety provides nature with insurance against extinction. It provides the primary way of insuring survival of a species and is one of the most powerful lessons that we can learn from nature.

Constantly changing environments demand change or extinction. That is why all living things have changed in the past and must continue to evolve. We know that horses at one time had five toes, then they had three, and today only one. We know humans have larger brains and smaller teeth than they did one million years ago. Interestingly, our teeth and our brains are both smaller than in our caveman days, a mere 10,000 years ago. A study of the earth reveals life forms that exist today but which did not exist in the past as well as life forms that used to live but no longer exist. Any species or organization that exists for any amount of time must be able to change its biological makeup if it is to continue to exist.

Evolution is the process by which life-forms pass on genes that are well suited to survive a particular environment. We tend to think of humans as somewhat special and above the lowly creatures of nature, but nothing could be farther from the truth. We know humans evolved from apelike creatures, but this was not a unique or special case. True, we are unique, just as other species are unique, but the mechanics of becoming human and interacting in our environment is largely due to natural selection and the gradual change in our genes. Natural selection still continues to push life and demands that all individuals in a species be expendable. It is nature's way of insuring survival of the species. It has been summarized as *genetics proposes, nature disposes.*

## DARWIN'S EVOLUTION

The value of the process was first recognized by an economist named Thomas Malthus (1766–1834) who wrote an essay on population. He was concerned about how population sizes kept stable and began noticing that more individuals are born into an animal species than can ever possibly survive to reach maturity. He reasoned that high mortality was good because without it, animal populations would grow too large to be supported by their environments. For example, many fish produce thousands of eggs in a single year. If we falsely assumed that fish breed only once and if we further assumed that only half survived and that each of these fish only weighed a few grams, then the total weight of just these fictional fish could, within a few generations, exceed that of our sun!

Charles Darwin, after reading Malthus's essay, wondered if the choice of which young individuals reached adulthood depended on their ability to survive. If all animals varied, as he had discovered, then could some of these variations better adapt them to survive and pass on those variations to the next generation? Variations that could not adapt to their environment were *selected out*. Darwin would later term this concept *natural selection*. To better understand natural selection, think of life as producing different features that the environment either chooses or rejects. A changing world needs such a device so that new and useful features can be passed on.

One of the best illustrations of the concept of natural selection involves a species called the peppered moths. They come in two distinct colors, dark and light. Early observers in England noted that about 99 percent in this species were light rather than dark. Light moths are better camouflaged on tree trunks. Blending in means they would be less likely to be eaten by birds. Later during England's Industrial Revolution, naturalists noted that dark moths increased dramatically from one percent to almost 90 percent.

Massive industrialization in England had also brought massive pollution so trees became darker in color because of soot. The light moths were now at a disadvantage and dark moths were selected for. With the passage of antipollution laws, England's environment began to recover. Less soot meant the light-colored moths had a better chance to survive and their numbers began to recover. Biological traits are not innately good or bad but rather their usefulness depends on one's environment (Relethford 1990, 23).

The goal of natural selection is simple. Each organism within Mother Nature is evolving in order to survive in its own little niche of the world. This is a primary reason why all species, including us and our groups and organizations, continue to seek to improve our competitive advantage.

## EVOLUTION AND CREATIVITY

It has been observed that only one in seven ideas reach the market (Gobeli and Brown 1993). It is better to generate more than enough ideas so that some of them can be wrong, than to be right by having no ideas at all (Lattimer and Winitsky 1984). It is not essential, of course, to come up with drop-dead new products, but it is essential to continually innovate even with older established products. To do that requires a Darwinian approach to ideas. A natural selection of the most fit ideas requires that far more ideas be generated than could ever possibly be of use. Those that stand the test of scrutiny will eventually be the most useful. The objective of a Darwinian approach to ideas was succinctly described by Fry, the *Post-it® Note* inventor, when he said, "You need thousands of ideas to have one or two successes in the end." This Darwinian approach to creativity helps to insure that some ideas will survive and, in turn, encourages piggybacking, in which other ideas are born in the process of analyzing ideas. It also helps to create a fertile climate for generating ideas as well as helps to encourage people to continue to produce a wide range of ideas.

> CREATE MORE IDEAS THAN YOU CAN POSSIBLY NEED

*Sword in the Stone,* the children's classic, has a tale that is worth telling to anyone hoping to stay competitive and understand evolution. In the book, the badger is trying to explain why man became master of all earth's animals. All of life's embryos look about the same. The badger theorizes that when God made them he called all of them before him and asked each to think about what they wanted. He offered each a gift of altering any parts of themselves into something that would be useful in later life. Each of the embryos thought it over and then made their request. The badger, for instance, asked for a thick skin, a mouth that could be used for a weapon, and garden forks for arms. Everyone specialized in one form or another. On the sixth day, God finally got to the last embryo—man.

## THE BADGER'S LESSON

Man's response was different than all the others. He said, "Please, God, I think that you have made me in the shape which I have for a reason best known to you, and it would not be right to change." God then congratulated man on being the only one to solve his riddle. Adaptability is far better than specialization. Man could learn and could adapt to changes in the environment, and that was his secret to success.

Darwin, like the lesson from the *Sword in the Stone,* is telling us that we must continually *acquire new behaviors* in order to survive. New behaviors are hard for anyone to learn, but behavior will change when the need is strong enough. Some early human behavior may not have been particularly well suited for our anatomy, but fossil evidence shows our own ancestors were able to modify their behavior because they were adaptive.

Many manufacturers and service companies understand this power of adaptability. Flexible manufacturing systems (FMS) and computerized robots are used to help factories churn out a wide variety of products. Other companies are in various stages of overhauling their information systems and reengineering their methods of developing new products so they can rapidly respond to changing consumer needs.

Using such leading-edge technology can be expensive and risky. In order to understand how to best create new ideas and innovations, we need to first look at how nature creates its new innovations.

## THE OTHER THREE FORCES

The first force of evolution, natural selection, receives all of the evolutionary publicity, but there are actually four forces that nature uses to create new prototypes and concepts. Each of these four concepts, alone or in combinations with each other, can dramatically increase our ability to create. These forces of nature that are applicable to creativity are: natural selection, gene flow (be same), genetic drift (be different), and mutation (be innovative and really different). Together they cause the changes that produce evolution. In biological species, the gene is the vehicle for change and adaptation. Natural selection is the way that Mother Nature chooses who wins and who loses. The process has led to a great deal of variety.

### VALUE MUTATIONS

A Stanford University professor, William Brian Arthur, notes the importance of nature's innovation that we call *mutations*. He says that every living cell, at the molecular level, is astonishingly alike. But a tiny, almost undetectable change in the genetic blueprint can be enough to produce an enormous change in the organism. A few molecular shifts here and there might be enough to make the difference between brown or blue eyes, between a gymnast and a sumo wrestler, and between good health and sickle-cell anemia (Waldrop 1992, 30).

All the innovations we see in life are due to the diversity in the structure of an organism's genes, which then affects how that species will function within its environment. These mutations are random changes in an organism's genetic code that are passed on to offspring. They are random because the process does not occur as a response to an organism's needs. It has been theorized that changes in DNA in the past were caused in part by environmental factors like background radiation from planet Earth. Changes in modern times may also be caused by heat and substances like caffeine.

When we think of mutations, some conjure up images of exotic creatures. One such creature actually existed. He was Brza (Quick Death) Smrt, a Bulgarian boxer whose name is pronounced Berzha Shmert. His boxing career spanned from 1234 to 1250. He was almost 7 feet tall, had arms that hung down to his knees, and was born without fingers, which made his hands natural clubs. He was estimated to weigh 350 pounds and had tendons in his arms and wrists as thick as those found in the legs of large elk.

His boxing style was simple. He would throw one punch and his opponent went down. Not only out, but dead. His first three fights ended before they began because he killed his opponents during the weigh-in ceremonies. Authorities eventually banned Smrt from fighting because they feared he might decimate Bulgaria's male population (Royko 1996). Thank goodness such human mutations are extremely rare, but far more subtle and far more frequent mutations are a natural part of human evolution.

Estimates indicate that spontaneous mutations in nature occur at a rate of about 1 in 100,000 to 1 in 1,000,000 sex cells. That does not sound like diversity until you realize that there are a vast number of genes in our bodies, in the order of 100,000 per cell. Roughly one out of every 20 sex cells or 5 percent carries a mutated gene, so there is a large probability that many people have mutated genes (Weiss 1995, 43). We do not notice them because the vast majority are not visible to the naked eye—but they are still there. It is a good thing because variety insures adaptability.

## THE LOGIC OF DIVERSITY

For 50 years, scientists have developed antibiotics like penicillin and streptomycin drugs that kill certain microbes. Their research has saved untold lives but it is only a temporary victory in a war that never ends. Widespread use of antibiotics (a force that changes the bug's environment) eventually leads to the evolution of a strain that is resistant to those drugs. Bacteria, like all living things, contains mutant genes, which allow them to survive antibiotic forces. These antibiotics, from the viewpoint of microbes, represent a catastrophic force creating untold disaster within its species. Mutation is their insurance policy against extinction. New mutations quickly become very common because those without the helpful gene are quickly killed.

For example, consider a man who is famous among his friends for running to the doctor to get medicine every time he thinks he *might* get sick. Most of his friends chuckle and shake their heads. But one of his buddies was galled by this display to the point that he once told him, "It is people like you that are going to create a microbe that will kill us all!" They both laughed when he said it, but the statement might not be too far from the truth. Years of exposure to penicillin has caused syphilis strains that actually flourish in it. Evolution protects all life, including microbes. As such, it means that these life-forms will eventually become resistant to any specific antibody. That is one reason why physicians, unlike my friend's doctor, are reluctant to prescribe antibiotics every time someone has an infection. Physicians have evolutionary knowledge and know if a drug is used to treat minor infections then it can eventually lead to microbes that resist treatment.

Nature's organisms do not somehow sense a need to change and then create a desired change. If, as chance would have it, random mutations do not produce the appropriate variation, then natural selection will not have the raw material needed to respond to adverse changes. Nature should be reminding us that, when there is no variation, there can be no selection and no chance of evolution or survival. Organizations tempt fate when they do not evolve or mutate. Those that remain the same cannot evolve and thus cannot survive. The vehicle for a biological species is its genes; for an organization it is its ideas and collective behavior. English biologist Richard Dawkins coined the term *meme* to identify a unit of transmitted cultural information analogous to a gene in biological evolution (Mann 1994, 242).

Richard Dawkins has shown that an interconnected group or system of ideas or memes can quickly develop its own agenda. He has said that he assigns no higher motive to this cultural entity than the primitive biological drive to reproduce itself and change its environment to promote its spread. Psychobiologists E. O. Wilson and Charles Lumsden have used some mathematical models and came up with their *thousand-year rule*. They estimate that cultural evolution can have significant genetic changes only about every thousand years. They say that genes and cultures are inseparably linked. Changes in one affect the other. Wilson also believes that change will not take place in a culture unless the genes are flexible enough to assimilate the change. Some believe that culture rewires biology, and that culture produces organisms that are biologically better able to produce, learn, and adapt in cultural ways rather than biological ones (Kelly 1994, 360–61).

## GENETIC DRIFT

Genetic drift, which is the random fluctuations of gene frequencies, is the way nature mutates and adapts, but it can only occur under certain conditions. This process has the most effect on gene frequencies from generation to generation, when the size of the breeding population is small. A good example of the potential for genetic drift would be a box containing equal amounts of blue and white beads. By chance you might get 50 blue and 50 white beads, but you are also likely to not have equal amounts. This founder effect shows that the smaller the number of founders (gene pool), the less the deviation.

In 1816, the English established a small garrison on a small island in the Atlantic Ocean called Tristan da Cunha. When they left, one man and woman were joined by a small group of settlers. There is little doubt that this small group would not normally contain all the genetic variation in their former larger population. Over time, the population on the island remained small and was even reduced due to emigration and disaster to a maximum population of 300. There was considerable chance for genetic drift. Genetic drift's general tendency is to reduce variation *within* a group. Drift decreases variability in a small population but also increases variability among different populations. Because drift is primarily effective within small populations, it was probably of greater significance in our hunter-gatherer past.

## TO INNOVATE—IMPOSE ISOLATION

Genetic drift is a force that causes variation among groups or departments within an organization. This variation in ideas and techniques can help to produce the *pockets of radicalism* so essential to creativity. The down side is the same as the up side, namely the variability it creates. It is cohesion and order versus creativity and innovativeness.

If an organization and its members rigidly follow standard operating procedures, look alike, and think alike, then cohesion will be strong but creativity and innovation will be weak. In fact, several researchers have confirmed that creativity is enhanced whenever individuals and teams have relatively high autonomy in the day-to-day conduct of their work (Bailyn 1985). Creative organizations do not try to imprint rigid behaviors but rather accept and even encourage new behaviors, actions, and ideas. But even this is not enough. Creativity in nature and in business does not exist unless genetic drift is present, but that alone is not enough. **Opportunity** and **motive** must also be present.

Motive usually occurs when there is some adverse change in the works. People will favor the status quo until forced to change, so it is often adversity that brings about change. Opportunity occurs when someone or a group has been isolated from a larger population. Small groups are subject to different selection pressures so there is a motive to change. Project teams or skunk works, who are trying to bring a new product on line, employ many of the same processes because they are isolated from the larger group (opportunity) without the traditional restrictions and have a motive for change (reducing product development time). Creative organizations that encourage pockets of radicalism will at least have subculture material that may be better adapted to changes brought on by outside forces.

The degree of cohesion versus creativity needed depends on your business environment. If it is stable and unchanging, then there is very little need for mutant or creative behavior or ideas. The more your competition, market, consumer, supply, or other economic forces change, the more you need to create a gene or more accurately an "idea pool" so you can remain in the creativity zone. (Take the Innovative IQ Survey, which is Exercise #5 in chapter 14, to find out if your organization's level of creativity is adequate for your work environment.)

# CREATIVITY THROUGH ADVERSITY

Genetic drift tends to create variety, and this variety, in turn, encourages new ideas and behavior. Both the opportunity and a reason or motive for genetic drift must be present. The opportunity for thinking divergently often comes from isolation or separation from this control. Adversity is frequently the motive for change and thus an essential partner in the dance that is genetic drift. A good example of how adversity can encourage creative thinking comes from the Japanese.

The Japanese have had the very good fortune to have misfortune. They have few natural resources, little land, crowded conditions, hot and humid summers, and after World War II, few capital resources. They did, however, respect education and were willing to cooperate with each other. Looking back, is there any wonder that they were likely to become a global power? Your potential, with all that against you, is unlimited. Research has shown that workload pressures that were considered extreme could undermine creativity. However, they also showed that some degree of pressure, some adversity, could have a positive influence if it was perceived as arising from the urgent, intellectually challenging nature of the problem (Amabile and Gryskiewicz 1987).

There would be little need for change or innovative problem solving, if nature or a business climate were unchanging or stable. Natural selection, mutations, and genetic drift are only useful when an environment is changing. Changes, though, mean you either adapt or die. Some adversity forces you to change, to struggle, and eventually to come up with a better way. No one likes to struggle or lose, but sometimes it is this very struggle that makes us better.

Probably nothing could have helped Japan or Germany more than losing World War II. They were given a chance to rebuild and given just enough help. It was an opportunity, not a gift. Gifts never help competitiveness, but just enough adversity and opportunity can create greater competitiveness.

---

### IF YOU WANT INNOVATION, CREATE MANAGEABLE ADVERSITY

---

The Japanese penetrated international residential air conditioner markets by manufacturing compact and quiet units. Look at what they had going for them. They had hot and humid summers and their homes were small and tightly packed. A bulky and noisy air conditioner would simply not be accepted by their consumers. High energy costs would also inspire them to pioneer energy-saving equipment. Clearly, one message of Darwinism is to be aware of your enemies with the greatest adversity; they can evolve into your most fierce competition.

Business's response to adversity, as with Mother Nature's response to adversity, comes from the necessity of becoming inventive in order to survive. That was the case with the Japanese, and it was the case with Southwest Airlines. Their approach to adversity is a little different than most airlines. When problems arise, many in their industry simply raise fares. Southwest felt that they had to keep their fares low and still provide excellent service. Such adversity forced them to rethink many of their services—like the need to serve meals (Freiberg and Freiberg 1996, 29). At one time they had only three airplanes so rather than buy more or cut back on their schedule, they tried something different. They could use the same number of planes and continue to improve their schedule if they reduced their turnaround time for an airplane at the gate to 10 minutes or less—that is loading, unloading, and pulling back from the gate in 10 minutes. No one in the industry thought they could do it. But they brought their fastest guys in to show others how to change a tire, check the oil, and get the plane turned around in 10 minutes (Freiberg and Freiberg 1996, 34).

## STRETCH GOALS AND INNOVATION

The Chinese word for crisis is two characters meaning danger and opportunity. Adversity is such a crisis that can help people move into the creativity zone. Competition pushes business to improve their competitiveness. It pushes us to think in new ways. Customers continually raise their expectations and force us to come up with new approaches. Cost and suppliers can create their own crises. The unimaginative sees the danger but reacts too slowly. The imaginative sees a crisis as an opportunity to sharpen competitive instinct and create new and better approaches.

Quad/Graphics is a $600 million privately held company with an annual growth rate of 10 to 15 percent. They are known throughout their industry for cutting-edge quality and innovation. Their chairman, Harry Quadracchi says, "Change is our bread and butter." He illustrated the principle of genetic drift when he stated, "There is virtually no similarity to the way every department is running today to six months ago" (Harari 1996). One of the secrets of their ability to innovate is letting their people set *impossible* goals (like 70 percent reduction in cycle time). The goals become possible if those same people are allowed the freedom and accountability to redo existing systems.

Jack Welch, the CEO of General Electric (GE), knows the value of adversity. He has been quoted as saying that managing in a difficult environment trains you a hell of a lot better than riding the wave of success. When the ship is going down, everyone knows to get out their lifeboats (Welch 1993). History shows that Welch was right. We need to feel some sense of urgency to insure cooperation. The more serious the threat or challenge, the more we focus our energies.

Creative people do not wait for a crisis; they create their own adversity. They do this by trying to satisfy their most picky customer. They seek to compete against the best in the world. They try to find the highest standards and the most severe restraints, and use them as their measuring stick. Frequently, organizations, including GE, have used stretch goals that far exceed normal expectation to also create a sense of adversity and challenge within the organization. If it is reasonable to assume a 2 percent growth, then a stretch goal to 10 percent. Adversity is the engine that helps to drive our need to adapt and change.

Another of those companies that sees the advantage of adversity is 3M. They believe that their stretch goals are imperative to their ability to innovate. Such goals help them to make the quantum improvements necessary to maintain their competitiveness. Although 3M has several of these stretch goals, two of them relate directly to innovation. The first one states that 30 percent of all sales should come from products introduced in the past four years. To further increase the sense of urgency, they added another stretch goal. This one says that 10 percent of 3M sales must come from products that have been in the market for just one year.

Equally famous is their demand that 25 percent of sales should come from products introduced in the last five years plus 10 percent growth in sales and earnings, 20 percent return on equity, and 27 percent return on capital employed. Just as important is the corresponding support systems needed to meet these goals. This includes seed money, mechanisms for linking employees (for example, E-mail) and conviction by management (Nemeth 1997).

## CREATING ADVERSITY

Stretch goals are not for everyone, but some measure of adversity is essential to spur creativity. Sometimes we can find adversity in very high standards. Michael Porter in his book *The Competitive Advantage of Nations* points out that many U.S. consumers will tolerate many products and services that would not be tolerated by Japanese or German consumers (Porter 1990, 522). Demanding consumers are the opportunity and motive that make us more innovative. Porter emphasizes the importance of tough customers and recommends selling to the most sophisticated and demanding buyers. He points out that industry exports increased substantially *only* when the domestic market became mature. Management should seek out buyers with the most difficult needs. They should establish norms exceeding the toughest regulatory hurdles (Porter 1990, 585).

German firms owe a great deal of their success to their demanding domestic consumers. Their customers tend to keep their durable goods longer than U.S. customers and maintain them better. Buying on credit is rare. When customers pay in cash, they often have a stronger concern for durability and expect higher quality.

### SEEK QUANTUM IMPROVEMENTS

To encourage innovation, 3M also uses adversity by trying to satisfy potential customers who have *exceedingly high standards*. The typical company might try to satisfy what 3M calls their lead users. These are people with high demands and this might predict where a product category is going. For example, 3M sells abrasives to the furniture industry and they try to keep in touch with those trends. However, they feel they might find out more about trends in finishing wood from guitar or violin makers because they have the most exacting requirements. It is these people who often need products that don't exist yet and so help to point the way to the future (Coyne 1996). William E. Coyne, Senior Vice President of Research and Development at 3M, says if you are interested in delivering microscopic amounts of a liquid for medical application, you might talk to people who manufacture the pumps for inkjet printers. If you want to work on the next generation of medical imaging devices, you'll probably talk to radiologists. However, you might learn more if you sit down with people who enhance images from interplanetary space probes. To innovate, you need to push yourself to go beyond incremental improvements. You need to force yourself to make quantum improvements, not incremental ones (Coyne 1996).

GE's management has also been able to inject adversity into their organization by focusing on these quantum improvements through a process called Six Sigma. It is a process most often associated with and pioneered by Motorola. The object is to define, measure, analyze, improve, and control your process so there are virtually no defects. Statistically speaking, as of 1998, GE currently produces 22,750 defects per million opportunities. The goal of Six Sigma is to reduce those defects to 3.4 per million processes, be it making the base of a lightbulb, lending money, or underwriting an insurance policy (Henry 1998).

Management at GE makes sure everyone gets the message about Six Sigma when they say it is quickly becoming part of the genetic code of their future leadership. In fact, training for it is an ironclad prerequisite for promotion to any professional or managerial position—and a requirement for receiving any award of stock options. Senior management compensation is heavily weighted toward Six Sigma commitment. Their experts in Six Sigma, whom they call Black Belts or Master Black Belts, are the most sought-after candidates for senior leadership jobs in the company (General Electric 1997).

## CREATE ADAPTIVE CHALLENGES

Ronald Heifetz, a professor at Harvard Kennedy School of Government, says leaders should help people find their own way through *adaptive challenges,* which are problems without readily apparent solutions (Sherman 1995). Steve Kerr, General Electric's director of their Crotonville plant, takes it a step further and says GE spends $300 million annually on formal training, but that they do not rely on course work to produce their leaders. Their courses are not the key. When GE asks people to write down the outstanding development experiences of their lives, only 10 percent cite formal training. The majority of peak learning experiences occur on the job and through serendipity, not planning. Kerr says you are more likely to get lucky if you *give people a carefully thought-out series of challenging work assignments* characterized by a great amount of responsibility and real risk taking.

The effect of self-imposed adaptive challenge was seen when Steve Jobs of Apple Computer challenged the Macintosh project team to completely rethink personal computer features. He contemplated the role of computers in society and began to believe they could have the same transformative impact that telephones had in an earlier period. While studying telephones in houses and offices, he noticed that they often sat on telephone books. This observation convinced him that the new MAC computer should have the same basic dimensions. This provided a difficult challenge because it required the layout of the interior of the computer to be done in a vertical rather than a horizontal manner (Nonoka and Kenney 1995). The outcome was a more compact and distinctive design.

If you do not naturally think of creating challenging work assignments or think like Steve Jobs—who does—then maybe you can tap another source of adaptive challenge. Consultant David Israel Rosen says one way to get breakthrough ideas is to talk to your, what chapter 4 called, lead users. For him, there are those who live in the future of his industry (Forsythe 1990). He emphasizes that, in a few years, most of your customers will be doing business the way lead users are doing it today. Rosen explained the concept by saying, "Suppose the Ice Age were coming back—what opportunities would that create?" His answer was to go to Siberia because Siberians do a brilliant job dealing with the cold. Lead users are the resourceful Siberians in every field (Forsythe 1990).

Finding lead users is a way of creating those healthy and stressful challenges that are needed to encourage creativity. The degree of stress needed depends upon how it is perceived. Levels of adrenaline and noradrenaline tend to increase when we react to difficult situations as challenges. Arousal actually strengthens us to handle further challenges if we have a sufficient break between challenges and if they are not continuous. *The deciding factor appears to be whether we see a solution to a problem and see ourselves as capable of resolving it.* In behavioral terms, it depends on who is in charge of the contingencies. Am I helpless or do I have some control over the situation (Caine and Caine 1994, 72)?

# IDEA FLOW

Gene flow or admixture is the last evolutionary force that helps species avoid extinction. It involves the movement of genes from one population to another and tends to bring a sense of order and stability. It is the tie that binds individuals to their species. This evolutionary force helps to insure that genetic material is shared with several separate populations. The greater the sharing, the more two separate populations will be genetically the same. This is accomplished through migration and interbreeding as individuals from one breeding population leave to join another. Culture serves the same purpose within organizations and society.

Distant geography provides barriers in nature that can reduce gene flow because it reduces the likelihood of mating. So too can different social and cultural patterns reduce the idea flow within the organization. With gene flow, the effect of immigration of new genes or the genetic make-up of a population is directly related to the size of that population. The same is true for memes idea flow. Small companies are also more likely to be affected by new ideas than larger ones. Both new ideas or genes can have dramatic effects on small populations, whereas large populations can absorb large amounts of this new information before there is a noticeable change in the population. Gene flow normally acts to reduce differences between groups, but it can also introduce new genes into a group.

Earlier we mentioned Richard Dawkins's system of ideas or *meme* as a counterpoint to genes. There are many ways to encourage gene flow's counterpart, meme. For instance, Monsanto has established what it calls a technology council to aid in the spread of this meme. It is comprised of top researchers from each of its various divisions. The council helps scientists swap ideas and thereby avoid duplicating costly research efforts (Nurturing 1989).

Richard N. Knowles, plant manager at E.I. DuPont De Nemours and Company at Belle, West Virginia, provides another example of how information flow works to improve their creativity. It is this information flow that makes it easier for you to cross the zone between the status quo and creativity, thereby encouraging new, beneficial innovations. Knowles notes that his plant's fixed costs have been reduced by about 19 percent, productivity is up 25 percent to 50 percent (varying according to product line), and earnings per employee have more than doubled. The reasons he cites for these improvements include—improving their technology, having a stronger focus on their vision and mission, and (perhaps surprisingly saying) opening themselves up to the spontaneous forces of nature. He emphasizes that organizations are living systems and the more you look at them that way, the more you see these natural forces taking place.

His plant did this by spending a great deal of time communicating with each other, their customers, their businesses, and their community. They felt that it was vital that each understood their vision, mission, principles, and standards of performance and did this by regularly sharing information on their business's performance. People were free to ask any questions they wanted. Nothing was off-limits except for personal or medical information. The goal was to try to answer all questions as promptly as they could, usually on the spot or in a few days at most (Knowles 1995, 57).

The value of sharing as many ideas as possible has been amply demonstrated by many innovative organizations. For example, 3M believes that their products belong to their divisions but their technologies belong to the company. Personnel at 3M are obliged to share any new exciting technology or even an interesting insight with their counterparts throughout the company. J. Marc Adams, Vice President of Marketing at 3M, says, "Our scientists know that one of our criteria for advancement is that a scientist has contributed to the growth of several divisions" (Adams 1997). This can only be accomplished by sharing and promoting technologies throughout the company.

# A DOUBLE-EDGED SWORD

Information or meme flow can also be enhanced through the use of teams, but there is also a risk with the tool. Nowhere is that risk better seen than at Apple Computers. The company began work on a computer that, according to Steve Jobs, would be "insanely great." The Macintosh team consisted of 25 close-knit members. The small size of the group worked in its favor because each member was responsible for a fairly large portion of the total design. Members freely consulted with other members when considering alternatives (Nonoka and Kenney 1995). Information flow within the group was also enhanced through organizational retreats away from the office. For as long as two days, up to 25 team members would discuss the project. The MAC team also occupied a building that was physically separate from the rest of the corporation. Such an environment led to intense and constant interaction, which was good, but just as importantly the separation led to conflict (genetic drift) with the rest of the organization. As a result, there was little transfer of technology or coordination between the MAC group and the other divisions of Apple.

Unlike Apple, 3M and E.I. DuPont were trying to enhance their idea flow by trying to become a *you need to know this* organization. The plant manager at E.I. DuPont says his people have learned to sift through the information and select what is most appropriate for them. Management does not try to decide who needs to know something but rather lets each person decide for themselves. In this manner, they are able to create a gene or idea pool while still creating homogeneity within the organization. It is this process of frequently communicating new ideas or information that acts like gene flow by rapidly spreading the new beneficial meme.

John Case would call this information or idea flow *open book* management. This occurs when everyone has immediate access to real information including strategic updates, income statements, balance sheets, sales and quality data, and current status of customers, suppliers, and partners. The more rapidly people can access critical information, the faster they can add to the idea pool, and the more innovative their decisions will be (Harari 1996).

GE's management believes a key to their corporate success has been directly related to this information flow. They believe they have a learning, sharing, and action-driven culture. Upper management believes this information flow across their diverse businesses gives them a true advantage over single-industry companies. Sharing information across their 250 diverse and global business segments is what they call *horizontal learning*. It is this sharing of a steady flow of new ideas among business that, they feel, allows them to continually raise the overall company bar for performance. Information flow is encouraged through compensation and reward systems. Originally, they used to reward originating ideas and standout performance with bonuses and salary. Now these bonuses and salaries are rewards for finding and *sharing* of ideas even more than those that originated them (General Electric 1996). Their idea flow involves sharing stories of customers made more competitive, of credit card and mortgage application processes streamlined, of inventories reduced, and factories performing better.

Information can be shared in both high- and low-tech ways, ranging from local area networks, expert systems, interactive newsletters, bulletin boards, and so on. The important point is to continue to create this horizontal learning. Creativity is most likely if information, resources, and expertise can flow smoothly from one area to the next. It is a lesson that even the most successful can forget.

Edward Lawler at University of Southern California notes that IBM probably invested the most of any organization in developing executive talent, but they taught people about a world that no longer exists. They were a company near the edge of rigid order in a world that demanded more fluid responses. They shrank their gene pool down to people who were very good at managing for the 1970s—so when the 1990s arrived, IBM had many people who were very good at the wrong thing. IBM is not alone; it is all too easy to forget the importance nature places on adaptation, evolution, and a creativity response to the outside world.

# SUMMARY

Two billion years ago, DNA became segregated into a nucleus of cells, instead of just being strung around inside us as it is in bacteria. The first partnership in earth's life occurred soon after creatures, resembling today's amoeba, became multicellular and invented a new trick—development. By five hundred million years ago, most of the major kinds of life that currently exist had appeared. By 120 million years ago, insects, dinosaurs, and mammals had evolved, and not just a few different kinds but a vast range of species. Now there was enormous diversity. Warm-blooded animals have dominated for only 40 million years; big-brained mammals have been around only for 20 million years. Our own specialization, really big brains, has been around only for a couple of million years.

Human civilization is only a few thousand years old, and most of our organizations only last a few decades. Nature's laws tell us the way it is—not how we would like it to be. The reality is that we must constantly innovate and change if we hope to remain viable within a changing environment.

It seems unlikely that it is coincidence that the two periods of greatest climate change, one around seven to four million years ago and the other three to two million years ago, also happen to be the precise two periods of greatest human change (Caird 1994). Great adversity creates great change and innovation. It forces us to adapt or die. Creativity and innovation come from the need to overcome adversity.

Any successful person or organization must be able to change. If more dynamic change is an essential part of your climate, then position yourself more in the creative zone by allowing greater diversity in ideas and approaches. To do that will require innovation and understanding and applying the four evolutionary forces. If new approaches are needed, then allow genetic drift. Provide both the opportunity and motive for change. Create isolation, seek to avoid homogeneity, and create minicultures and new gene or idea pools. If your business environment is more stable and unchanging, then focus on control and sameness. This does not mean no change, but rather focus on effective order. This means coming up with beneficial hierarchies. Improving a sense of predictability while maintaining the status quo can also have competitive advantage because people need to feel they have a sense of direction. (See chapter 6 for other ways of enhancing performance in a stable environment.)

# REFERENCES

Adams, J. Marc. 1997. Competing in highly dynamic markets by strategic innovation: The 3M model. *1997 McGill Graduate Business,* 13 February, 13, 18.

Amabile, T. M., and Gryskiewicz, S. S. 1987. *Creativity in the R & D laboratory.* Technical Report No. 30. Greensboro, N.C.: Center for Creative Leadership.

Bailyn, L. 1985. Autonomy in the industrial R & D laboratory. *Human Resource Management,* no. 24, 129–46.

Caine, Renate Nummela, and Geoffrey Caine. 1986. *Making connections.* New York: Addison-Wesley.

Caird, Rod. 1994. *Ape man.* New York: Macmillan.

Coyne, William E. 1996. Building a tradition of innovation. *UK Innovation Lecture,* 5 May, 6.

Forsythe, J. 1990. Breakthrough ideas. *Success* 37, no. 8 (October): 38.

Freiberg, Kevin, and Jackie Freiberg. 1996. *Nuts! Southwest Airlines' crazy recipe for business and personal success.* Austin, Tex.: Bard Press, Inc., 34.

General Electric. 1996. *1996 Annual Report* (reprint), 2.

General Electric. 1997. *1997 Annual Report* (reprint), 5.

Gobeli, David H., and Daniel J. Brown. 1993. Improving process innovation. *Research-Technology Management* 36, no. 2 (March-April): 38.

Harari, Oren. 1996. Mind matters. *Management Review* 85, no. 1 (January): 47, 48.

Henry, David. 1998. GE's Welch sees opportunity in Asia crises. *USA Today Money Section* (reprint), 27 February.

Kelly, Kevin. 1994. *Out of control.* New York: Addison-Wesley Publishing Company.

Knowles, Richard N. 1995. Expanding the growth of self-organizing systems. *Journal for Quality and Participation* 18, no. 3 (June): 56–57.

Lattimer, Robert L., and Marvin L. Winitsky. 1984. Unleashing creativity. *Management World* 13 (April/May): 22–24.

Mann, Murray-Gell. 1994. *The quark and the jaguar.* New York: W. H. Freeman and Company.

Nemeth, Charlan Jeanne. 1997. Managing innovation: When less is more (creativity in management). *California Management Review* 40, no. 1 (fall): 69.

Nonoka, Ikujiro, and Martin Kenney. 1995. Towards a new theory of innovation management. *IEEE Engineering Management Review* 23, no. 2: 3–7.

Nurturing those ideas. 1989 *Business Week,* no. 3110 (16 June): 107.

Porter, Michael. 1990. *The competitive advantage of nations.* New York: The Free Press.

Relethford, John H. 1990. *The human species: An introduction to biological anthropology.* Mountain View, Cal.: Mayfield Pub. Co.

Royko, Mike. 1996. 13th century boxer would have left Ali without head. *The News-Leader,* 6 June, 8A.

Sherman, Stratford. 1995. How tomorrow's best leaders are learning their stuff. *Fortune* 132, no. 11, (27 December): 90–96.

Waldrop, M. Mitchell. 1992. *Complexity: The emerging science at the edge of order and chaos.* New York: Simon & Schuster.

Weiss, Mark L. 1995. *Human biology and behavior: an anthropological perspective,* 3d ed. Boston: Little, Brown and Co.

Welch, John F. 1993. A master class in radical change. *Fortune* 128, no. 15 (13 December): 83.

# CHAPTER 6

# Operating Below the Zone:
# Confucianism's Lessons for Management

## INTRODUCTION

Most of this book is designed to encourage innovative thinking. Such thinking is needed in a world of change, but there can be too much creative energy and change. It is a matter of matching your creative needs to your environment. Some environments require constant adaptation, change, and innovative thinking; others put a premium on stability and order. This chapter is for the latter, those who desire some creativity and change but operate in a fairly stable business environment. Confucius had some help for those in this situation. He believed in structured order and felt there was a proper place for change. He emphasized tradition, proper behavior, obligation, and duty, and he believed in hierarchies. This chapter looks at how to use hierarchies and nature's pecking order to introduce structured change. Key points include the following:

- Showing people how the rules have changed
- Using lateral moves and zigzagging
- Needing to work in areas unrelated to your discipline or area
- Using creative hierarchies

Everyone, it seems, is always talking about the need to change and the need to innovate, but sometimes it is best to use caution. The Chinese word for business is *sheng-yi*. This word comes from two characters that mean "to give birth to ideas." Therefore, one would assume, that their business would be a very creative enterprise but this often is not the Asian reality. Singapore elder statesman, Lee Kuan Yew says that innovation, initiative, and creativity have no place in today's Asia; that only the top 3 percent to 5 percent of society can handle the free-for-all spirit of innovation. He says, "If the whole society becomes avant-garde, it will fall apart." Two Chinese sayings illustrate the importance of conformity: "It is the tall tree which catches the wind" and "It is the nail which sticks out most which gets pounded in first" (Swanson 1997).

Whether you agree with Lee Kuan Yew or not, most recognize that too much change and instability can produce as big a risk as too little. The simple fact is that it is the environment that determines how much change is needed. If your environment is stable, then do not overreact. Stability, as well as change, must be referenced in terms of what is needed to respond to your environment. If customer expectations, cost and competition, and outside forces are somewhat stable, then create a stable organization to match. Creativity and change need only be present to the degree that the environment demands it. Even environments in the middle of dynamic change do not do so in a chaotic manner. Things resist change for a reason. Change can be good, but organizations must create some sense of order; otherwise, they become chaotic. Organizational leaders can learn important lessons about order from the study of Confucianism. Michael Porter in his book *The Competitive Nation* noted the value of Confucianism to the competitiveness of some Oriental cultures. It places a high value on education, hard work, respect for authority, and achieving success by moving up a social ladder (Porter 1990, 465). Confucianism's overriding theme is one of order and of finding where you fit within the larger system. It emphasizes the value of an orderly life, attention to one's position in that life, and upward mobility by applying Confucianism principles.

Confucius lived during the time of disorder the Chinese call the Warring States (433–221 B.C.). He was a member of a somewhat obscure lesser noble clan and worked for a time as a minister of state, but his thoughts would dramatically affect one of Earth's oldest thriving cultures. He could not find a ruler to put his ideas about governance into practice so he turned to meditation and teaching. Confucius's philosophy presented a purified version of traditional Chinese practices. It emphasized personal integrity and disinterested service in a governing class. Not only did his teaching have a dramatic impact on China, but it also demonstrated both the power and danger of creating order.

Confucius's writing specifically advocated the *principle of structural order.* Although Europeans respected nobility, Confucius went farther. Everything had its correct place in the whole of experience, so the tendency of Confucianism was to support institutions likely to insure order. This included the family, hierarchies with their graded levels of obligations to superiorities. Those that later adopted Confucius's philosophy respected traditional culture, emphasized the need for proper behavior, and were drilled in their moral obligations to properly discharge their duties and meritocracy.

Confucius's impact on Chinese culture was cemented because generations of Chinese civil servants were later drilled in his precepts of behavior. His philosophy and the documents he produced provided an outline for proper governmental service and produced reliable, disinterested, and humane civil servants. The heart and soul of this philosophy were texts he was said to have compiled. To the Chinese, these writings were like the Old Testament. They were a miscellaneous collection of old poems, chronicles, and moral sayings later called the Book of Change, which was used for generations to mold civil servants and rulers. His concern was not supernatural but rather practical. Good order became more important to their culture than seeking assurance from dark gods (Roberts 1988, 152).

## CREATE STRUCTURED ORDER

Order alone is not enough to remain competitive, but it does provide some essentials for survival. Just as important, it gave many a place a sense of permanence and tradition. It is the kind of order that the *within-the-box* creative types mentioned in Chapter 3 require. In this secure environment many are able to express their own creativity. It also provides the kind of security that can even be essential to many *outside-the-box* types. (For more discussion of this topic, see Chapter 8.) China's emphasis on structured order also gave it a resilience that was unique to early civilizations. Although barbarian invasions occurred from time to time, but they did not damage the foundation of Chinese civilization. China's tradition of clans that linked many families was also a factor. However, the bureaucracy of civil servants trained in Confucianism survived centuries of disunion in imperial China and was the key to China's successful emergence from collapsing dynasties and competing states.

Chinese bureaucracy, more than any other institution, held their civilization together for two thousand years of change, and Confucianism was the centerpiece of this bureaucracy. Rote-memory learning of these moral principles was part of the civil servant examination. Those that sought administrative posts underwent examinations designed to show which candidates had the best grasp of the moral tradition of Confucianism, as well as to test mechanical abilities and the ability to perform under pressure. All in all, it created one of the most effective and ideologically homogeneous bureaucracies the world has ever seen.

The civil service also carried extrinsic rewards. Most civil servants came from the landowners but were set apart from them. They acquired a civil service office by successfully passing the examination and enjoyed a status just below imperial families. The office brought many material and social privileges. This bureaucracy rested on competition and learning as a way of social mobility. Their bureaucracy created a good order that helped the Chinese to resist changes from hordes of invaders. Their armies would lose but their culture remained intact. It helped them to avoid complete disorder and chaos and remain stable, but such a proposition is always a balancing act.

Establishing some degree of structured order and stability within an organization, just like in a culture, is necessary to avoid chaos and so much disorder that it hurts inventiveness. Such an approach works especially well in a stable environment, but it is one of those double-edged swords. Some structured order can be a good thing for creativity and competitiveness but when significant change does occur, order resists it just as ice resists changing its shape. Too much order can pose as big a problem as too little flexibility or creativity. A criticism was that the

Confucian philosophy led to a preoccupation with the past and ignored the need to explore, take risks, and change. The government's role, like so many modern organizations, was to oversee, consolidate, and conserve the order, not be innovative. The result was that Ancient China was at the edge of static order and remained stable almost to the point of immobility. Stability, security, and a premium on order can work well as long as environmental pressure to change does not become too severe.

# HIERARCHIES AND PECKING ORDERS

Hierarchies are everywhere in business. At one time GE had assigned all employees to one of 29 civil service style levels of rank. At headquarters, people within any given level worked in offices of almost identical size. People though continually seek order to better identify their own place. Even if offices are the same, people will find both obvious and subtle ways of determining who's on top. Almost identical size of offices at GE were not a problem, visitors to an office could and did calculate the square footage of an office by counting ceiling tiles and thus his or her status in the hierarchy (Tichy 1993).

Hierarchies and bureaucracies exist in large part because of our need for order and direction. All people and organizations crave direction and order. It is one of our most primal needs born from the need to maintain life. The search for creativity is by its nature filled with uncertainty and real risk, which runs contrary to our innate instincts. The more we understand where we are headed and how we are doing, the better we feel. For this reason, leaders are constantly struggling to keep their people focused with a sense of direction. We favor predictability and order over uncertainty and change. One way we do this is by creating hierarchies or pecking orders.

Norwegian naturalist Thorlief Schjelderup-Ebbe was one of the first to identify the so-called *pecking order* in animals. On his family farm he observed chickens and their barnyard behavior. The first thing he began to notice was how much order and decorum existed. When hens were fed, they were all hungry but none ran up and grabbed whatever she could. Rather, a somewhat regal hen first stepped up to the container of grain and started dining. Others would patiently watch, then slowly another would come forward, and so on.

After watching several times he discovered that the order these diners were taking was not arbitrary. Every day, the same bird went first, the same hen went second, and so forth. Whenever a strange chicken was tossed in the yard, the normally peaceful birds quarreled and fought. He reasoned that the stranger was trying to establish her position in the barnyard society. In the world of chickens, there is a social hierarchy. Other naturalists have discovered similar social pecking orders in a variety of species. Historians note similar artificial pecking orders throughout recorded history.

The desire of modern managers and leaders to reengineer and flatten our organizations and thus create more equitable relationships can never be completely successful if the desire is to eliminate all hierarchies. We may seek new and innovative work practices, but we will still need hierarchies; it has always been that way. In our earliest civilization we even ranked our gods.

Our deepest biological drive is the drive for dominance. Even though there may be flatter or more creative organizations in the twenty-first century, there will always be a need to express our need for hierarchies. The law of the jungle creates a need for survival, order, direction, and achievement, and new innovative work arrangements cannot ignore those needs. Flat organizations need ladders for achievement just as much as vertical ones do. There must be an *up* in our work to appeal to our innate hierarchical needs.

> ## THERE IS, HAS ALWAYS BEEN, AND ALWAYS WILL BE PECKING ORDERS, SO CREATE GOOD ONES

Organizations will continue to need to innovate and change, but how it is done is equally as important as doing it. The typical approach toward change is to try to reorganize by systematically flattening decision making and downsizing mid-level management. The theory is to focus on processes or customers rather than on the traditional functional hierarchy and thereby improve performance. The attempt is to empower lower-level people with greater responsibility and to create a more equitable culture. However, all of this should not lead us to believe that the hierarchy is dead (Horizontal 1995). Hierarchies are needed, maybe not in their present form, but it is our nature that gives us a natural desire to create them. Our animal relatives, chimpanzees, baboons, and apes, with whom we share the greatest number of social instincts and highest percentage of DNA, are all prisoners of their deep-rooted hierarchical drives. These nonhuman societies have dominant hierarchies within their societies that identify which individuals are least important and which are the most important.

Hierarchies serve a vital purpose and should not be eliminated. Even innovative work teams will naturally develop some kind of hierarchy. Hierarchies provide a sense of order, predictability, and stability that all creative humans seek. We seek certainty and our place in the hierarchy provides us with that order. We may need to flatten organizations, but we will always need to create hierarchies that give people a sense of order and direction.

# HIERARCHIES AND POETS

When you begin looking, it soon becomes obvious that hierarchies are in every fabric of our lives. Nobel prizes are listed with physics first, chemistry second, and physiology and medicine third. The physics prize is always awarded first at the beginning of the ceremony in Stockholm. Many seek equality but there still resides within all of us a natural biological and innate drive, a hierarchical drive that has been with us since early civilization. Howard Bloom, in his book *The Lucifer Principle,* notes that in the first century highborn citizens of the Roman Empire were obsessed with ambition and winning honors in the eyes of their compatriots by rising in the hierarchy. It was called the cursus honorarium or the "racecourse of honors." Once you landed a prized new post, you were able to work very, very hard so you could move up the next rung on the ladder.

You showed your worthiness to move up this ladder by a variety of attributes. Success depended on your diligence, on giving exceptional speeches in the forum, or on making donations of warships and monuments to the state and presentations at your own expense at massive public spectacles. If the crowd and those in power liked what you had done, you moved up the ladder. If you worked hard enough and were a little lucky, you might even attain the ultimate prize of becoming one of the two consuls. These were the highest officers in the land and the supreme commanders of the army. The hierarchy was an excellent motivator for Rome's best and brightest to dedicate almost all their energies for the betterment of society (Bloom 1995, 193).

Naturally, not everyone was happy with this hierarchical approach to life. The Roman poet Horace wrote that the struggle for power was vain and meaningless. In his poems, he said true beauty and happiness were found in the quiet moments of a private life in the countryside, a life isolated from the hustle and bustle of Rome. At least Horace was above the petty one-upmanship that dominated the racecourse of honors. Actually, he was excluded from it because it was only open to Romans of noble birth. Horace was the grandson of a slave, not an aristocrat. His father was a free man who had worked hard and had been able to send him to a school for the upper crust of Roman society. Horace continued to socialize with the elite after he graduated, but he still was not one of them. He could not have participated in their race for power, even if he had wanted to.

The idea that Horace created had a great deal of appeal. Gradually, generations of men who once looked forward to their race up the hierarchy became ashamed of their ambitions. Instead, they increasingly went to contemplate their souls. Rome's best and brightest were no longer interested in the race or the betterment of their state. Surely this must have been one of the reasons for Rome's gradual loss of vigor as its people shifted their energies to self-indulgence.

Creating pecking orders like Rome's racecourse of honors is not bad. It is only bad when what you are attempting to achieve is evil. Service to your culture or your society does not seem as bad as service purely to yourself. People should not be ashamed of ambition and of the need to achieve; it is a natural biological drive that we share with many of other animals. Studies of humans low on the pyramid show that there is an increase in blood pressure, heart attacks, and strokes, and a loss in "mental swiftness" (Tomoshok, Van Dyke, and Zegans 1983; Maser and Seligman 1977; Bower 1992). When you slip in the pecking order, it is a fall from which many never recover! Anyone who is seriously considering reorganization, change, and introduction of innovative workplaces must be acutely aware of the powerful emotional forces at work. Recognition is the first step in creating a truly effective change effort. Change often means that somebody loses or feels they are losing; somebody feels they are sliding down the ladder. Most will not take it well.

Most everyone knows of our natural desire for food, clothing, and shelter, but people also crave status and prestige. We crave to move up the pecking order. We can send food and medicine to the underprivileged in South America but, if you give them a chance, many will spend money on lipstick rather than food because it brings the admiring glances of men and the envy of women. In Harlem, teenagers' desires are often not for something practical but rather for status symbols. Often prestige means more than food, shelter, or clothing because we all want to move up the pecking order.

## USING THE POWER OF THE PECKING ORDER

Obviously, the workplace is going through fundamental change, but people remain the same. You can reengineer the corporation but only nature can reengineer the DNA code. Although the world is different than it was 100,000 years ago, our genetic code remains essentially the same as it was when our species lived in caves. You can develop innovative work arrangements, eliminate levels within the organization, and provide more empowered decision making, but people remain with the same basic biological desires. There is within all of us an innate need to climb the primal hierarchical ladder and to secure the power that usually goes with it. We have a need to achieve; it's not psychological—it's biological and it's instinctive. Even artists and poets like Horace have a personal need for power. As creatures of Mother Nature, we expect to find hierarchies. They have always been a part of our environment. Hierarchies were a tool that insured that the strongest and most fit of our species would survive. The biological need to move on a hierarchical ladder may be stronger in some than in others, but we all have it. If there is no way to climb the ladder, we, like Horance, create our own mental ladders. In modern societies, the criteria for survival may change but the need for a hierarchy remains.

> **SHOW HOW THE RULES (FOR SUCCESS) HAVE CHANGED**

The message of this chapter is simple. The world may change but people need predictability and order in their lives; few intentionally seek a chaotic environment. All of us, even the most outside-the-box types, want to feel like there is logic and order to our lives. Hierarchies help to satisfy our innate need for reasonable predictability, order, and direction that are the centerpiece of creative thinking. Admitting that hierarchies and order are important does not mean that things cannot be different. We may need some hierarchy but not the same old kind. We should not blindly accept the status quo—our hierarchies must also evolve. Hierarchies can never be eliminated, but often they must be changed to better match competitive needs. Humans, despite what we may say, do not seek equity; we seek in varying degrees, to win, to dominate. It is our nature. We cannot change our temperament that prefers the status quo and order over change nor can we turn off our quest for power and control. We can, however, refocus those efforts. All of us need a hierarchy, but it does not mean that you still have to play by the same old set of rules.

## NEW HIERARCHICAL MOTIVATORS

Organizations that have experimented with creating innovative work and decision-making arrangements have often left little room for upward mobility. What happens when the rules change and promotions and upward mobility no longer apply? Several organizations today are rethinking motivators and how they can begin to satisfy their personnel's innate hierarchical needs.

Today flatter, more empowered organizations mean that young managers must wait longer before getting a chance to exercise real authority. Many organizations are experimenting with reducing managerial layers while still trying to keep hierarchical motivators within the organization. Some organizations have reduced pay grades but then encouraged managers, from different disciplines, to make *lateral moves* by broadening responsibilities of many of their managerial positions including reducing the number of approvals needed before one can make decisions.

William L. McKnight, 3M's President, makes a point of encouraging innovation through policies like the 15 percent option and a dual-ladder system of promotion. Laboratory employees can advance up a technical ladder, as well as a management ladder, and continue to do what they do best—research and development (Mitsch 1990).

## TEACH AND REWARD ZIGZAGGING

Hierarchies need to be within all organizations so when there is no up, executives can zigzag or move back and forth across divisions and organizations. The reasoning for zigzagging is that moving through many areas or divisions enhances your knowledge and effectiveness, and it gives people the wider perspective that was advocated in chapters 3 and 4. One of the building blocks of creativity is the need to "expose the problem to other perspectives." Disney used their "seven-year itch" as a way of creating more innovative thinking. We need to feel that we are moving up the hierarchy, but up can also be sideways. Focusing our hierarchical needs on moving laterally not only broadens us, it also helps us to think in new ways and bring fresh perspectives to old problems.

Organizations in the past would move a person up through the organization until they eventually acquired a broader general management position. Creativity demands that we develop managers with a wider perspective. Increasingly, it is not uncommon for many managers to spend several years working in different areas before coming to one permanent department. Zigzagging will only be good for creativity and for the organization if those zigzaggers have a chance to grow through the experience.

## WORK IN AREAS UNRELATED TO YOUR OWN

Managerial cross-fertilization is a concept that has already been associated with innovative thinking. It helps to motivate and enhance an organization's creative potential by first bringing a wider perspective to a problem. It also encourages the "transfer of knowledge from other disciplines" so essential to creative insight. Cross-fertilization encourages teamwork by making each functional and departmental manager know what is involved in the other manager's job. A *creative hierarchy* would promote and reward those people who have their own responsibilities and also become knowledgeable of several other disciplines. In a hospital, for instance, a nursing supervisor could theoretically pitch in and help to run the material or inventory department or vice versa. Granted, each of us may not be able to do an expert job but we could, in a pinch, run another department.

People normally want to move up the hierarchy because they know that this is how you get ahead and make more money. But not every organization manages that way. The rules are different at Gore and Associates. Each of their employees is called an associate. Granted, there is nothing especially noteworthy about that, but it is how they treat their associates that is different. There is order, but they have erased some of the line that keeps things highly ordered. The ice has melted a little. There are no bosses at Gore, only team leaders, and every associate has a mentor. Associates meet every six months to rank peers by assessing their contribution to the group. Committees merge these lists and set raises, ranking low pay from the highest to the lowest. Anyone can and does take ideas and complaints to anyone else. W. L. Gore calls their style un-management. There are no company titles. Bill Gore says, "Leadership is a verb, not a noun. It is what you do, not who you are" (Huey 1994).

# SUMMARY

The publicity today is on change and innovation, but it must be a balancing act. Too much creativity or the wrong change can be just as bad as too little of it. We naturally crave some sense of stability and order in our lives. That is why we acquire routines. Stability is one of the most fundamental of our human desires. The real trick is to match our environmental needs.

Hierarchies, bureaucracy, and authority are often thought of in contempt in today's fast-paced society, but it is not a one-sided story. They all give an organization a sense of order and direction and provide a stability that can be beneficial.

It was not just the Romans who employed hierarchies. They have always been and will always be important to humans. We have always sought to order the universe around us. Adam labeled insects, fish, reptiles, birds, mammals and, finally, man in his world. Guess who was on top? The Catholic church ordered itself into a hierarchy: laity, priest, bishop, archbishop, pope, saints, and angels. In our earliest civilizations we even tended to rank our gods. Mesopotamia was one of the—if not the—earliest human civilizations. To each of their gods they assigned a role—there was the god of air, another for water, and so on. At the top of the hierarchy were three great male gods. Egypt was one of our earliest and best-known civilizations. The Egyptian kings were not simply kings but gods in human form. Under them was a hierarchy of bureaucrats.

Nations are not the only ones that will fight for their place on the hierarchy. History teaches us that there is a biological reason for this human behavior. One of our deepest drives is the biological drive for dominance that pushes us to climb the hierarchy. Although there may be more innovative organizations in the twenty-first century, there will always be a need to create ways of helping us express our hierarchical needs. We need predictability, order, and direction as much as we need a sense of freedom and creativity. Innovative work arrangements need ladders of achievement just as much as the old; vertical organizations need them because there must be an "up" for work to appeal to these innate desires. Without something to accomplish, some prize to acquire, we sit on our haunches. We evolved over millions of years and have been successful because we were adaptive and sought conquest and control of our environment. Hierarchies give us something to accomplish as well as provide a sense of order. They can be used to help define and reward the *right* kind of innovation.

The zone of creativity rests between rigid and highly structured order and disorganized and random chaos. Below the zone does not mean that we need no creativity. To the contrary, we need to make adaptations—even if they are more within the box improvements. Having motivators that build upon our innate desires helps to insure successful change. There is room for creative hierarchies, cross-fertilization, and zigzagging in even the most stable environment. Any species that does not encourage some diversity is ultimately at risk to any change—even if you are below the zone of creativity.

# REFERENCES

Begley, Sharon. 1997. How to build a baby's brain. *Newsweek* (spring/summer): 32.

Bloom, Howard. 1995. *The Lucifer principle,* New York: The Atlantic Monthly Press.

Bower, Bruce. 1992. Chronic hypertension may shrink brain. *Science News* 12 (September): 166.

Horizontal management to rule post-reengineering era. 1995. *Industrial Engineering* 17, no. 1 (January): 11.

Huey, John. 1994. The new post-heroic leadership. *Fortune* 129, 4 (21 February): 48.

Maser, Jack D., and Martin E. P. Seligman, eds. 1977. *Psychopathology: Experimental models.* San Francisco: W. H. Freeman & Co.

Mitsch, Robert A. 1990. Three roads to innovate. *The Journal of Business Strategy* 11, no. 5 (September–October): 19.

Porter, Michael E. 1990. *The Competitive Advantage of Nations.* New York: The Free Press.

Roberts, J. M. 1988. *History of the world.* London: Penguin Books.

Swanson, Lauren. 1997. A Chinese view of birthing and growing ideas. *Marketing News* 31, no. 7 (31 March): 17.

Tichy, Noel M., and Stratford Sherman. 1993. *Control your destiny or someone else will.* New York: Harper Business, 39.

Tomoshok, Lydia, Craig Van Dyke, and Leonard S. Zegans. 1983. *Emotions in health and illness: theoretical and research foundations.* London: Grume & Stratton, 76.

# CHAPTER 7

# In the Zone: The Panda Principle's Basics of Product and Process Innovation

## INTRODUCTION

This chapter examines how to best innovate. The advice sometimes runs contrary to our normal thinking. The Panda Principle tells us not to worry about being the best, rather be the first to gain an early advantage and move on. Change cannot be predicted, controlled, or managed, so be reactive. Recommendations for effective innovation include the following:

- Get there first
- Be aware of the sequence of events
- Be sensitive to change *outside* your domain
- Be aware of changing priorities

Research studies have found a connection between high levels of innovation and profit. Jeff Mauzy's 1993 study of 150 major U.S. firms found that innovative companies experience profit growth rates that were four times as great as those for non-innovative ones (Higgins 1996). The search of ways to innovate is perhaps the reason that many companies today are hiring liberal arts graduates. Many believe these people are better for today's business than MBAs. Lee Iacocca, former CEO of Chrysler has said, "MBAs know everything and understand nothing." He meant that most business graduates had formulas for everything but that those formulas were useless in an age in which creativity and innovation are essential to succeed (Zelinski 1989, 24). Creativity is essential to help produce more new products or services, make improvements in current products and services, make faster decisions, reduce costs, avoid threats, find new markets and new ways of promoting company services, and better differentiate your product from others. Several research studies support the belief that increased stock prices and earnings are tied directly to successful innovation through new product introduction. Companies that launch a steady stream of relatively successful new products and services over a long period of time often see their stock prices consistently rise (Kuczmarski 1996).

Motorola, 3M, Amgen, Owens-Corning, Rubbermaid, and Pfizer each spend more than 4 percent of sales annually on research and development (R and D) (Kuczmarski 1996). But it does not have to be that way. Innovation does not require tons of money. A Fortune analysis of 143 companies, comparing R-and-D expenditures as a percent of sales and rank on their list of innovative companies, shows very little correlation between R-and-D spending and standing on their list (O'Reilly 1997). For instance, they noted that the relationship between R-and-D dollars and perceived innovation can be quite perverse. Pharmacia Upjohn spends 18 percent of revenues on research, more than almost any company in any industry. But money does not make it right; they ranked as 339 in innovativeness in the year of the study. Their lack of R-and-D productivity is not unique among businesses. Eighty percent of executives surveyed replied that they thought innovation was critical to their company's future competitiveness, but only 4 percent indicated that their firms knew how to innovate in a superior way (Higgins 1996).

# LESSON ONE: THE PANDA PRINCIPLE

At one time there were alternatives to our present writing systems, counting systems, sets of number signs, and calendars. Some of these systems were undoubtedly better. So how did we end up with these? The answer to this question rests on how we go about innovating. Often the sequence of events is just as important as the actual inventions. The losers believed that they had a better mousetrap— sometimes they did, but they were fighting the Panda Principle. **Gain early advantage** should be the prime directive of any innovative organization.

William E. Coyne, Senior Vice President of Research and Development for 3M, is one who would believe in this prime directive. He believes that you get the most from your innovations if you move quickly. If a new project overspends its budget by 50 percent, it can shave profits by 4 percent. But if the product is six months late to the market, profits are trimmed by 33 percent. He says this shows better than anything else why they feel a sense of urgency (Coyne 1996).

For instance, consider the VHS and Betamax videocassette formats, which were introduced about the same time and therefore had equal market shares. A combination of luck and corporate maneuvering brought VHS vendors a slightly bigger early market share. Chaos theory tells us that often little things can make a big difference, and it was true in this case. Having a slightly bigger market share at the beginning gave VHS an enormous advantage in spite of it being inferior to Beta videotape technology. This small variation meant that more video stores stocked VHS prerecorded tapes, which cascaded into more customers choosing VHS recorders, which meant that VHS rapidly took command of the entire market. Betamax had a slightly better technology, but being better does not guarantee success. You can build a better mousetrap, but you had better do it **first.** If you have a choice between building a better product or getting a reasonably good product out first, you had better get there first. It is the *Panda Principle* in action.

Stephen Jay Gould in his book, *Bully for Brontosaurus,* shows the value nature places on being first in a new niche. He calls it the Panda Principle. Creatures in nature can survive perfectly well, even though other creatures could occupy their grid or niche more competitively. Companies that do not compete with the best can try to do what the panda did (Cohen and Stewart 1994, 322). The panda's "less-competitive" characteristic is its thumb. It is not a real thumb, it certainly is not as good a thumb as some potential competitors might have, but it is the best the panda could manage. The panda had already committed its fifth digit for other uses. Normally a more fit competitor would have driven the panda to extinction, but there is an exception to the eat-or-be-eaten rule. The panda population remains stable as long as a more fit competitor does not arrive. We all know that less-fit companies and managers do survive, sometimes for quite a while, as long as the conditions for survival are not too severe. This is a dangerous place to be, but sometimes you get lucky. Inertia is a great force for survival.

---

### GET THERE FIRST

---

An Italian named Pellegrino Turri constructed the first typewriter in 1808. Several dozen patents were filed, and prototypes were built over the next six decades, but none were mass produced or commercially successful until April 1874 when an American gun manufacturer, E. Remington & Sons, shipped its first *type writer,* based on a prototype by American inventor, Christopher Sholes. A great diversity of typewriters were tried out over the next 40 years. Thomas Edison even tried his hand at it. Some machines resembled pianos; some including Remington's resembled sewing machines (they were already making sewing machines—so why not?). Some used a ball carrier (like later-day IBM Selectric) that moved; others had moving type bars and, in some cases, even the machine moved. In some, ink was applied to a ribbon; others put it directly on the typeface. Keyboards were straight, curved, or circular, with one to nine keys. Sholes's system originally used piano keys in a single row, with letters in alphabetical order. He soon changed to the QWERTY arrangement, which is the standard keyboard we use today. Surprisingly, he chose it because of sluggish response! Sholes continued to innovate his product by adding type bars, an inked ribbon, and a cylindrical paper carriage.

The QWERTY keyboard is a perfect example of the Panda Principle of *getting there first.* Typewriter speed records are owned by a better-fit tool called the Dvorak simplified keyboard, but people still use the old, less-effective QWERTY keyboards, not because it is better but because it was there first. They enjoyed a head start as the keyboard of the first successful typewriter.

In those early days, both the typewriter and typist operated differently. Early typewriter keys often jammed. These jams were impossible to see because the keys were hidden from view below the roller. The problem could only be spotted after the typist had typed several lines. Those early typists used a different method than today's touch typing. They typed using one finger on each hand, so the QWERTY system forced them to slow down by making them use the left finger to type the most common letters.

Letters were positioned not for ease and speed but to slow the typist down so one key would have time to recede before the next one was hit. In addition, the top row contained all the letters needed to spell typewriter so the first typewriter salespeople could impress customers by quickly typing out the name of the new machine.

You might expect that the keyboard is designed so that most of the typing is on the home row. You would be wrong. Only 32 percent of strokes are on the home row; most (52 percent) are on the upper row and 16 percent are on the bottom row. No more than 100 English words can be typed without leaving the home row. A new version of the keyboard called the Dvorak has nine of the 12 most common English letters—including all five vowels and the most common consonants (T, H, N)—on the home row, while the six rarest letters (V, K, J, X, Q, and Z) are on the dreaded bottom row. Therefore, 70 percent of typing strokes remain on the home row, with only 22 percent on the upper row, and a mere 8 percent on the bottom row. Thousands of words can be typed with only the home row (Hoffman 1997).

The QWERTY system is an inferior method. Over 3,000 English words utilize the left hand alone. This overuse of one hand extends to our weaker fingers. The QWERTY makes almost as much use of the weakest finger (pinky) as it does of the second strongest (right third). The outcome of all of this is typing that is unnecessarily tiring, slow, inaccurate, hard to learn, and hard to remember. A good typist's fingers cover 20 miles on a QWERTY keyboard but only one mile on a Dvorak keyboard. Dvorak typists hold most world records for typing speed. QWERTY typists make about twice the errors that Dvorak typists make. A beginner using a QWERTY keyboard needs 56 hours of training in order to reach a speed of 40 words per minute. The same person needs only 18 hours using a Dvorak keyboard (Hoffman 1997). In short, the QWERTY keyboard is a perfect example of obsolete technology and process. So why do we use it? Why was it the winner?

The QWERTY typewriter did not win because it was the best invention then or now; rather it won for other reasons (Cohen and Stewart 1994, 323). The QWERTY system was clearly less "fit" or effective, but those buying the typewriter perceived it to be a better way. Because one company, E. Remington & Sons, started mass-producing a typewriter with the QWERTY layout, more typists began to learn the system, which meant that other typewriter companies began to offer the QWERTY keyboard (Order from Chaos 1994). Soon everyone began ordering this new tool and inertia built up. The power of the status quo took over, and Remington continued to use the QWERTY—even as newer typewriters evolved.

Being first is a powerful force. When the U.S. Navy faced a shortage of trained typists in World War II, it experimented with retraining QWERTY typists to use Dvorak. The retraining soon enabled Navy test typists to increase typing accuracy by 68 percent and their speed by 74 percent. Faced with convincing results, the Navy ordered thousands of Dvorak typewriters, but they never got them. The Treasury Department vetoed the Navy purchase, probably for the same reason that insured QWERTY success. There was inertia of tens of millions of typists, teachers, salespeople, office managers, and manufacturers. August Dvorak died in 1975, a bitter man. "I'm tired of trying to do something worthwhile for the human race," he complained. "They simply don't want to change" (Hoffman 1997).

Another case in which getting there first outweighed being best occurred in 1956. The United States was investigating a number of design proposals for its civilian nuclear power program. There were reactors cooled by gas, by ordinary *light* water, by a more exotic fluid known as *heavy* water, and even by liquid sodium. In hindsight, many engineers believe that high temperature gas-cooled systems would have been much safer and more efficient. So what happened? In October 1957, the Soviets launched Sputnik. President Eisenhower became very eager to get any reactor up and running. At that time, the only reactor anywhere having any inertia of being ready was the highly compact, high-powered version of the light water reactor developed by the Navy for their nuclear submarines. The Navy hurriedly scaled the reactor up to commercial size and placed it in operation. All of this led to further technical developments and by the mid-1960s, it had basically displaced all others in the United States (Waldrop 1992, 41). Getting there first should be the top priority for anyone who hopes to be competitive.

The Panda Principle makes displacing an old product or service in business a hard task. It can also provide hope for us but only if we move quickly. Darwin tells us that the best competitor among those not too different from it will win. We do not always need to be world class, but we do need to be fast, fast at innovating. The Panda Principle tells us to not worry so much about having the best product or service, rather having a reasonably good one that was developed early will create a great deal of inertia. Waiting to become the best means waiting at the altar. Create, innovate, and move *now*! We will figure out how to perfect the moves later.

## BEING VIGILANT

Being first helps, but it is not an iron-clad insurance policy against extinction. The panda could become extinct if it fails to keep better adaptive predators out or fails to continue to evolve. Fish in the Riff Valley in Africa existed for generations, but when the perch was introduced, this more-fit competitor wiped out all less-fit ones. The same is true of organizations. General Motors was here first and has a lot of inertia. Things were okay until new foreign competitors changed the rules and their chances for survival. It is lucky for the QWERTY keyboard and General Motors that business, like nature, seeks stability and order; otherwise, things would really be chaotic.

A business person cannot simply try to be the first. He or she must keep a vigilant eye on change. Often it is not the size of the change but rather the ongoing sequence of events that is essential. Little changes can and do produce large consequences.

Stuart Kauffman points out that if you were to take a patch of prairie and put a fence around it so that certain types of small animals can no longer enter the plot, then the plot will change over time. The interesting part is when the fence is removed. Because the same set of animals return, it would seem logical that the original community of plants would return—but they do not. What you get is a different stable community (Kauffman 1995, 211). Once you are out of the game, it is hard to get back in because someone will take up your space. Being successful, it seems, is dependent not only on who gets there first and creating inertia, but also on the *sequence of events*. Successful innovation depends not only on who came first but also on who or what came after the innovation. Not only do you have to look forward, you also have to look behind you.

In the 1890s, when the automotive industry was still in its infancy, gasoline was considered the least-promising power source. The Panda Principle was working well for steam, which was well developed, familiar, and safe. Gasoline, on the other hand, was noisy, dangerously explosive, and hard to obtain in the right grade. But gasoline did win out, largely because of a series of historical accidents that may have slowed steam's inertia. In 1895, a horseless-carriage competition sponsored by the Chicago Times-Herald was won by a gasoline engine. This significant event probably inspired Ransom Olds's 1896 patent of the gasoline engine and subsequent mass-production of the "Curved-Dash Olds." This all helped gasoline engines overcome its slow start and gain some inertia of its own, but the fatal blow to steam came from an unexpected place. In 1914 there was an outbreak of hoof-and-mouth disease in North America. Outbreak of the disease led to the withdrawal of horse troughs, which were the only places where steam cars could *fill up* with water. By that time the Stanley Steamer and its condenser and boiler system was invented so steam cars did not need to be filled up every 30 or 40 miles; but it was too late. Steam never recovered, and gasoline quickly became locked in (Waldrop 1992, 41). If things had been different, if steam had won, or if there had not been an outbreak, then it is likely outcomes would have changed. The sequence of events is important, which is why it is so important to remain sensitive to changes both within and outside your domain.

3M calls this sensitivity to one's environment foresight, or figuring out where their customers are going. Innovating in the right way requires knowing what their customer needs are and what trends are affecting their industries. They want to know both articulated customer needs as well as unarticulated ones. The latter are harder to find, but often lead to the most rewarding products. 3M notes that the world's first masking tape and the Post-it® Note were not products asked for by their customers (Adams 1997).

## BE SENSITIVE TO SMALL CHANGES IN YOUR ENVIRONMENT

It is easy to get into a market first, but as more and more enter, it becomes harder to survive. Eventually, a market niche becomes saturated and stable and no further competitors can be added. Studies by Kauffman show the interdependent nature of environments. Change a single entity and small or large avalanches of extinction can and do occur (Kauffman 1995, 217). The most important thing we can do is to continually seek ways of monitoring direct and indirect environmental changes so we can pick up any changing priorities.

## WHAT ARE THE PRIORITIES?

Changing priorities have always shifted the balance of power in nations as well as in nature. In the early sixteenth century, Magellan, a Portuguese explorer, made a voyage around the world. It demonstrated that all the oceans were interconnected. From this time on, the priority changed. European nations with access to the Atlantic would have opportunities denied to landlocked powers of central Europe and the Mediterranean. It meant Spain and Portugal powers would now be joined by France, Holland, and, above all, England. Sometimes priorities are changed by a single historical event like Magellan's voyage. At other times, the event can be as simple as a change in government regulations.

If you have extra time, look at an old map of natural gas pipelines crisscrossing the United States. An ignorant person would simply see a cobweb of interconnections capable of shipping gas from any gas field to any local company. Those in Washington and in utilities would not see it that way. Government regulations required a gas pipeline to run single-mindedly from a specific field to a particular utility company—with very few shifts or diversions (O'Reilly 1997). Then along came a person named Kenneth Lay of Enron.

In 1986, his company had just been formed by a merger of two natural gas giants. The Texas oil company executive had been trained as an economist and recognized that Enron could use all those natural gas lines as a network to buy gas where it was cheap and sell when it was needed. All he needed was a little deregulation. That was opposite thinking of other gas utilities who were vigorously resisting deregulation. When deregulation did come, Enron hired aggressive well-paid traders and almost single-handedly began creating spot markets. His gas business colleagues said there was no need for spot markets. Enron found that its new approach could reduce the cost of gas for some utilities by 30 percent to 50 percent. Priorities changed, so the company created new products, new services, new kinds of contracts, and new ways of pricing. Gas used to cost a lot—new, cheap, free-market gas meant new opportunities. Lay did the unthinkable; he used gas for fuel in electric generation plants—something forbidden under old federal regulations. To prove their point, Enron operated their own gas-fired power plant in Texas, showing that it competed economically with coal-fired plants with far less pollution (O'Reilly 1997, 62).

# SUMMARY

Being sensitive to changes and their potential effects encourages innovative thinking. When it comes to innovation, it is usually the quick or the dead. It won't always work, but it is far better to get to the market first with a second-rate product or service than to get there second with a first-rate product. That's the Panda Principle in action.

Being first does not insure success. It is often the sequence of events surrounding an innovation that is just as important as the innovation. Even the order of events matters. Replay events surrounding an innovation and change one sequence, and you could change reality. Change cannot be predicted, controlled, or managed. Therefore, it is better to be reactive than retroactive. It is better to be flexible and adaptive than strategic. Keep on innovating because you never know when a little change will produce large consequences.

It is essential to know your innovative IQ and the stability or dynamics of your work environment. Assess your degree of creativity and ask if it is enough to keep you competitive. The questionnaire (Exercise #5 in chapter 14) can help show your innovative potential by looking at several areas—cultural, decision making, organizational structure, and control issues—and by examining how you respond to them. Among other areas it also examines your sensitivity to changing priorities in your customers, competition, cost, labor, technological, and outside factors. It, or similar tools, can help you to identify how flexible and innovative you are and compare these results to your business climate. Many will find that they need to enhance their creativity and ability to respond to changes. Most will find it valuable to have a better understanding of their unique environmental demands. Being sensitive to them is essential for survival and to make sure your workplace creativity meets or exceeds those environmental demands.

# REFERENCES

Adams, J. Marc 1997. Competing in highly dynamic markets by strategic innovation: The 3M model. *1997 McGill Graduate Business Conference* (13 February): 6, 7.

Cohen, Jack, and Ian Stewart. 1994. *The collapse of chaos: Discovering simplicity in a complex world.* New York: Viking Press.

Coyne, William E. 1996. Building a tradition of innovation. *UK Innovation Lecture,* 5 May.

Higgins, James. 1996. Achieving core competence—It's as easy as 1, 2, 3 . . . 47, 48, 49. *Business Horizons* 39, no. 2 (March–April): 27.

Hoffman, Paul. 1997. Queer typewriter, oy! *Discover* 18, no. 4 (April): 34–41.

Kauffman, Stuart. 1995. *At home in the universe: The search for law of self-organization and complexity.* New York: Oxford University Press.

Kuczmarski, Thomas D. 1996. Creating an innovative mind-set. *Management Review* 85, no. 11 (November): 48.

Order from chaos. 1994. *Management Today* (November): 64.

Waldrop, M. Mitchell. 1992. *Complexity: The emerging science at the edge of order and chaos.* New York: Simon & Schuster.

Zelinski, Ernest J. 1989. Creativity training for business. *Canadian Manager* 14, no. 2 (summer): 24.

# CHAPTER 8

# Risk Taking, Innovation, and Product Development

## INTRODUCTION

Research has consistently shown the value of encouraging risk taking in creative endeavors. Doing things differently and finding new ways of producing products and process depend on taking chances. People naturally tend to do what they have always done because it is safe. Innovative thinking occurs most easily when people feel *free to fail*. It is essential to develop an atmosphere of risk taking by doing the following:

- Not accepting the status quo
- Asking why, before asking how
- Separating responsibility and accountability
- Identifying long-term cost of the status quo
- Nurturing risk taking

Evolve or become extinct is the iron rule of biology, and it pretty much applies to all of us. This planet and life on it has gone through both subtle and catastrophic changes in its four billion year existence. In the modern world, it has been estimated that a species becomes extinct every 20 minutes. You either change or die, so too is it with modern organizations. Herb Kelleher, CEO of Southwest Airlines, has said, "A company is never more vulnerable to complacency than when it's at the height of its success" (Freiberg and Freiberg 1996, 60). It has always been that way and it always will be. As much as we would like to stop overcoming adversity, stop exploring new opportunities, or stop taking chances, we cannot. Through exploration, we learn how to adapt to inevitable changes. When we are successful, we know this; but when we slip down the hierarchy, our instincts for survival take over and we grow more conservative rather than exploratory. This is a behavior we share with many other creatures.

When birds are hungry and desperate for food, you might think that they would sample everything they run across. With starvation at hand, some good-looking berry might be the key to survival. But hungry birds do not nibble at every unusual-looking item to see if it can be turned into a meal. Fear of the unfamiliar renders them conservatives. Birds that benefit from a bonanza of food are very different. They strut around with full stomachs, not ignoring morsels they come across but rather ready for a potential adventure in dining. The logic is that exploring unknowns is a risk. A hungry bird, like a marginal business, cannot take the chance of being immobilized for a day or two by food poisoning; those with stored-up calories can afford to experiment.

In times of trouble, societies and organizations act in similar ways. They tend to shun the new, even if it means future erosion of their ability to compete. When the Turkish empire was crumbling in the sixteenth century, authorities were sure they could recapture former glories by returning to traditions of the past. Europeans came up with improved ways to prevent plagues but the Turks refused them. Why? Foreign techniques departed from customs that had once made Turkey great. Companies and markets in a state of decline will respond in a similar manner. It is what brain researchers often call *downshifting*.

Perceived threats "narrow our perceptual field," so we revert to status quo thinking. Researchers Caine and Caine note that we downshift, we revert to the tried and true, and follow old beliefs and behaviors regardless of what information the road signs provide. Our responses become more automatic and limited. We are less able to access all that we know or see what is really there. We also seem less able to engage in complex intellectual tasks, those requiring creativity and the ability to engage in open-ended thinking and questioning. It also appears to reduce our ability to see the interconnectedness or interrelationships required by thematic or ecological thought processes (Caine and Caine 1994, 69–70).

## KEEP YOUR EYE ON THE BALL

Michael Eisner, CEO of Disney, notes that the principal asset of their organization is creativity. In trying to describe what it takes to be a creative company, he related a story he heard about the legendary baseball player, Babe Ruth. A reporter once asked Ruth, "How is it that you always come through in the clutch? How is it that you come up to bat in the bottom of the ninth, in a key game with the score tied, with thousands of fans screaming in the stadium, with millions listening on the radio, the entire game on the line, and deliver the game-winning hit?" Ruth's answer, "I don't know. I just keep my eye on the ball."

Eisner says that keeping one's eye on the ball is, for him, a metaphor for what we must do in a creative company. In this case, it is to keep focused on creativity. They create products that people want. They create products that people cannot even know they want until they have bought a ticket or tuned in. Disney does a pretty good job of keeping its eye on the ball. The percentage of new products they introduce each year is in the 20 to 30 percent range or 80 to 90 percent in film and television. Eisner says they introduce one or more new products every week of every year (Eisner 1996).

---

## DON'T ACCEPT THE STATUS QUO

---

When it comes to change, Disney is the exception; the rule may be Boeing. Lee Tom Perry says Boeing illustrates a common strategy of many organizations. Boeing made a decision to delay development of a hypersonic transport despite the fact that their engineers had completed initial designs for the hypersonic transport that would fly six times as fast as the Concorde. The $12 billion price tag for development cost frightened management. The company decided to wait until Airbus or another competitor had plans for its own hypersonic transport *before* further developing the technology. This risk-adverse strategy is a departure from the company's early risk-taking history.

In 1952 Boeing bet $16 million, which was most of its net worth, on an innovative prototype passenger jet when the market was dominated by Douglas Aircraft's propeller-driven DC series. Propeller planes became obsolete because of Boeing's bold move. Past CEO, Frank Shrontz, said that Boeing did not want to get into the position of Douglas Aircraft, which at the beginning of the jet age became complacent about their product line. He said Douglas was unwilling to take the risk, so someone else did. Shrontz was, however, not talking about their hypersonic transport. Rather he was referring to investing in developing their 767-X, a 350-seat plane with only a slightly longer range than Boeing 747—not five times longer like the hypersonic transport. Perry notes that with $4 billion in cash, little debt, and an $80 billion backlog in orders for commercial airlines, Boeing may be letting a golden opportunity pass it by. Boeing has gone from high risk to high complacency (Perry 1995). Many organizations, like Boeing, operate under the belief that stability and predictability are a good thing. Such an approach certainly gives you greater control over the organization and produces more consistent responses but creativity suffers.

Research shows that being able to develop new products is a powerful way a business can grow and that the most successful types of new products are the truly innovative ones, rather than line extensions or minor improvements. But managers and organizations, like Boeing, tend to avoid risk taking for many reasons, often because they are afraid of the risk. It is called risk-averse settings (Reed 1991, 356).

## DO YOU FEEL SAFE TO FAIL?

Using stretch goals, Six Sigma, or setting exceedingly high standards—from an organizational point of view—is almost a prescription for failure or success, depending on your outlook. Jack Welch, CEO of G.E., emphasizes that the trick is not to punish those who fall short. If they improve, reward them even if they haven't reached the goal (Welch 1993).

Research studies show a strong relationship between the encouragement of risk taking and creativity (Amabile 1996). Such an attitude was demonstrated when Robert Johnson, of Johnson and Johnson, is reputed to have congratulated a manager who lost money on a failed new product by saying, "If you are making mistakes, that means you are making decisions and taking risks" (Nemeth 1997).

Demanding exceedingly high expectations requires a high tolerance to failure, risk taking, and liberal management where anything goes. To achieve such extraordinary measures requires continually innovating. Following nature's pattern, many parts of the old ways of doing things will quickly become extinct. The remainder will be smaller and better prepared to compete. It requires long-term commitment, not squeezing out profits at the destruction of other vital concerns of the organization. Using stretch goals, for instance, that focus on long-term profitability and market share may not sit well with shareholders who want a bigger dividend—now! Rapid improvement, as stretch goals infer, demands long-term commitment. You should not starve vital parts of the organization by squeezing out profits, which could have been used to insure long-term survivability. Tolerance for failure not only applies to the way you run a business. It also is applicable to how to manage people.

Michael Eisner says a company like Disney must create an atmosphere in which people feel safe to fail. This means forming an organization in which failure is not only tolerated, but fear of criticism for submitting a foolish idea is abolished. Creativity is hurt if people become too cautious. Eisner believes that if people are afraid to speak up, afraid to rock the boat, afraid of being ridiculed, then potentially brilliant ideas are never uttered—and never heard. It was Wayne Gretsky, the great hockey player, who said, "You miss 100 percent of the shots you never take" (Eisner 1996, 5).

Disney's CEO does not want failure to become a habit, but they do want their people not to be fearful and take chances. One of the ways they try to do this is through what their executives call their Gong Show. The executives would meet and toss ideas around. Anyone who wanted to pitch an idea to the executives could do it. Rank had no privilege. Each time there are about 40 presenters. Eisner says for it to work requires that each presenter feel safe about giving their ideas. The idea is not to pull their punches but to also give full and serious consideration to each idea. They will tell people if they think an idea won't work. But they also tell them why and how it might be improved. Of course, they also tell them when the idea has promise.

Disney's executives believe that creativity is enhanced if you take the time to listen and be honest in your reactions. It is important to be open and to recognize that ideas come in all shapes and sizes. Your people must believe that if they have an idea and can express it, it will be fairly considered. Eisner says this is more than employee relations. This is supported by the fact that some of their better ideas have come from these Gong Show presentations. An essential part of this creative process is also having an organization that can follow through and execute those good ideas (Eisner 1996, 7).

Research shows that the building blocks for increased innovation and new product success include those like Disney's top management commitment and a desire to take risks as well as a compensation program that rewards new product performance. Studies on innovation identified several factors associated with new product success including open-mindedness, supportive and professional management, as well as good market knowledge, a superior product that meets customer demand, good communication, and proficiency in technological activities.

Open-mindedness toward risk taking is essential to success in new product development. Complacency is a primary reason that many soon lose their competitive edge. Researchers have shown that highly innovative products do especially well in terms of profitability, capturing domestic and foreign market share, and meeting sales and profit objectives. Meanwhile, non-innovative products including modifications, revisions, cost reductions, and repositionings do well in terms of return-on-investments and domestic market share. They run second to highly innovative products on the other performance measures. It was the moderate or middle-of-the-road innovative products that fared poorly.

# MANAGERIAL RADICALISM

Innovation and risk taking require overcoming our natural tendency to prefer the status quo. Nature has no such problem because it *does things differently.* Darwin's evolutionary insights, as seen in chapter 5, demonstrate the significance mutations play in the survival of the species. There would be no life if life could not adapt. The primary way nature is able to do this is through mutations. The ability of species to mutate insures survival of the species, and the same is true of organizations and their leaders. Nature never and business rarely operate in a static or rigidly unchanging state.

Simon Caulkin, editor of the Observer, notes that in an era of change, monolithic upper management will likely fail to generate the creativity needed to give the company adequate options. His point is that diversity of opinion and approach are needed to fight consensus (Caulkin 1995). Straight-ahead thinking, without occasional side roads, dooms one to immobility. Honda, recognizing the value of non-linear thinking, hires groups of managers in mid-career from other organizations with the express aim of introducing challenge and contention into the company. Ralph Stacey, professor of management at the Business School of Hertfordshire University, calls this **creative destruction**. It involves eliminating old, comfortable concepts and paradigms and embracing new ones (Order from chaos 1994).

William McKnight, a chairperson from 3M, says ". . . men and women to whom we delegate authority and responsibility . . . are going to want to do their jobs in their own way . . . mistakes will be made, but if a person is essentially right, the mistake he or she makes is not as serious in the long run as the mistakes management will make if it is dictatorial and undertakes to tell those under its authority exactly how they must do their job" (Coyne 1996). This is the philosophy that the company takes to heart. 3M believes that you need to be tolerant of initiative and tolerant of the mistakes that occur because of that initiative. The company's rule that allows all technical employees to devote 15 percent of their time to a project of their own choosing is designed to institutionalize a bit of rebellion in their labs. This 15 percent *slack time* allows their people the opportunity to explore to take risk.

3M acknowledges that failure is a part of life and that they expect failure on a grand scale. In a bit of logic that has the appeal of Darwin's natural selection, he says for every 1,000 raw ideas, only 100 are written up as formal proposals at the company. Furthermore, only a fraction of those become product ventures. And over half of their new products fail (Coyne 1996).

# RISK TAKING AND THE STATUS QUO

Robust and spontaneous order exists everywhere in nature, but so too does disorder. Humans, like other creatures, try to control their environment, and they often do it in the most familiar way—by not changing. As noted earlier, we prefer the order and the status quo, even when it's really, really bad. In a number of studies by Barry Shaw, participants played the role of a financial officer who was faced with improving profitability. They were asked to allocate R-and-D funds to one of the company's two operating divisions. After they received feedback about the performance of each division, they were again asked to make a second allocation of funds. Shaw's research showed that when participants received negative information about the performance of their chosen division, they would do a strange thing. They would then make an even bigger allocation to that same division! It was a bigger allocation than those made by participants whose first choice was performing satisfactorily (Silver and Mitchell 1990).

Such a response is a common reaction. Managers continue to stick to their existing way of doing things, and recommit resources to poorly performing divisions rather than put those resources into other opportunities. In another case, Shaw had participants play the part of a vice president of human resources who had two choices involving downsizing. One plan would save one of their three plants and 2,000 of their 6,000 jobs. In the other plan, you had a one-third probability of saving all 6,000 jobs but also had a two-thirds probability of saving none of the plants and none of the jobs. Half of the participants received information that indicated the first plan (2,000 jobs) had been implemented during a previous crisis. The other half received information that it was the second plan, not the first, that had been the preferred plan in the last crisis. The study demonstrated that participants most often selected the plan designated as the status quo. It is almost instinctive for people to crave order and hold on to the tried and true. Bad jobs, bad marriages, poor diet and exercise habits all display our tendency toward the status quo, predictability, routine, and order. It is safe and sure, even if it's not the best.

We often do not choose the best among alternatives, nor do we try to maximize but rather prefer to do what we always have done. A recent survey of 300 upper-level managers by Lee Roy Beach and Terence Mitchell shows that making decisions depends on three different kinds of information. The decision has to fit within certain guiding principles, beliefs, values, or morals. In other words, choice is indexed in terms of "who we are" (for example, we produce quality products). Decisions are also made in terms of "where do we want to go." Normally decision-makers also have some *ideal* or mental picture of something they are trying to attain (for example, we need to adopt a team approach to improve our quality). Finally, decisions are made about "how we want to do it" and "what will be the outcome." This process includes plans or tactics for reaching the goal as well as predictions of the expected result (for example, we did this before and it worked pretty well).

These mental images are not focused on maximizing something but rather are images about how the world should be in relation to a decision-maker's guiding principles. Leaders make decisions based on what they think are likely outcomes. Once a decision is made, we often follow it with either a "how are we doing" or "what should we do next" decision. New actions or decisions usually concern the next step, "where do we want to go next." Normally, new actions must be compatible with these previous decisions. The typical choice then becomes determining the best course of action from a limited number of alternatives. Such a choice depends on its *reasonableness* or compatibility with our underlying morals, ethics, and so on.

---

ASK "WHAT SHOULD WE DO?" BEFORE ASKING "HOW ARE WE DOING?"

---

The weakness of the human decision-making process is that we often ask "how are we doing" before we ask "what should we do" (Silver and Mitchell 1990). It is only when we realize that things are not going very well that we begin to look at new, alternative ways of doing things. We are unlikely to change course as long as we are receiving positive feedback about our decision. We are only likely to change what we do if our goal has changed and if we realize what we are doing is not compatible with it. We will change if it looks like our action will fail, but we do resist accepting negative feedback. In his book *Quitting,* Dale Dauten interviewed hundreds of people. He reported that people who believe the status quo might actually get better almost never changed their course of action (Silver and Mitchell 1990). It often takes strong adversity to force innovative approaches.

Risk taking is not natural for a species that prefers the status quo, so how do you overcome it? The first step is to understand how people perceive consequences and actions. People report feeling stronger regret for bad outcomes that are the consequences of new actions than they do for similar bad consequences that result from remaining with the status quo (Silver and Mitchell 1990, 42). For instance, a manager may remain with a reliable but expensive wholesaler if the reliability and cost of using a new one are uncertain. It is the fear of making a change and having it turn out badly that keeps the manager from acting. We will do almost anything to avoid change. If things are going badly, we will even lower our goal to fit the situation so we can keep the hope of having success with the status quo.

---

TO ENCOURAGE INNOVATION, SEPARATE RESPONSIBILITY
AND ACCOUNTABILITY

---

Because people tend to naturally evaluate how they are doing before looking at what they should do, we need to establish some artificial behaviors. We need to find a way that forces us to sample alternative choices or decisions. One good way to avoid the normal resistance is to separate the responsibility for generating and examining new alternatives. Other departments can propose an idea, but let R and D or other groups have the responsibility for actually examining new alternatives. The Apple Macintosh was created this way. Steven Jobs, Chairman of the Board at Apple, created a separate team to develop a new computer by pulling people from their normal duties at Apple and putting them together in a garage. The result was the Macintosh (Silver and Mitchell 1990, 43).

> ## IDENTIFY LONG-TERM COST OF THE STATUS QUO

Focusing people on the long-term costs versus short-term gains can be a way to create greater risk taking. Developing scenarios and forecasts based on the potential long-term costs or consequence of maintaining the status quo helps to keep you focused on the need to change (Exercise #9 on storyboarding in chapter 14 can be used for this purpose). We always retain the hope that we can stay with the status quo. The tendency is even stronger if we expect strong negative consequences like losing our job if the status quo plan fails.

# NURTURE RISK TAKING

Andrew S. Grove is CEO of Intel Corporation. His organization is successful and many share in his perceptions of reality. But he and those that think like him have made a serious mistake. To his credit, he notes that the world now operates as one big market and that every employee competes with every person in the world who is capable of doing the same job. He goes on to also state that many of those competitors are very hungry. It is a cold world that he paints, one where it is adapt or die. He feels that employees should recognize that they are in a business in which nobody owes you a career. He then encourages people to accept these realities and to start soul searching by asking themselves if they are contributing (Grove 1995).

Grove's comments clearly show that he understands the nature of business and that he appreciates its competitive demand, but he and other senior officials make a grave error. The knowledge that you are on your own is probably not news to most working men and women. What is probably little appreciated by senior officers is that the "new" competitive realities cannot eclipse the fact that people have powerful nurturing needs. Like it or not, the reality is that most of us need constant nurturing, need to be listened to, and need to receive pats on the back. We need a sense of security and not to feel that we are throw-away containers. People, despite competitive realities, will always need a sense of order and permanence. If you want people to shape up, you can use fear, threats, and reality checks. If you want them to be innovative and apply their creative skills, then you need to make them feel that they are important, valued, and nurtured. Starving birds do not take chances. They try to avoid risks, not embrace them.

```
SHOW COMMITMENT AND CARING TO EMPLOYEES
```

Michael Porter, author of *Competitive Nations,* recommends a competitive strategy that flies in the face of many "you are on your own" companies. He notes that his research has consistently pointed out the value of treating employees as permanent. Underinvestment in training and development has always been a risky proposition. The risk in today's era of do or die is especially acute. Porter notes that many have criticized the United States because its employees do not seem committed to their company or their profession. He feels that the reason for this apathy is, in large part, due to companies not being committed to their employees (Porter 1990, 528).

# NURTURING PHILOSOPHY

Nurturing entails more than simple training and education—it is attitude. One company and its leaders that has taken this nurturing philosophy to heart with great success is Federal Express or FedEx. This organization employs 110,000 employees and is the king of overnight mail delivery. Their revenue in 1995 was $9.4 billion, up 11 percent from 1994. Net income over that same time period was also up from $94 million to $298 million. Earnings per share in 1995 was $5.27, up 44 percent from the previous year. This company, in more ways than one, is on the move because of their people first philosophy.

FedEx makes sure that employees have an opportunity to give feedback and to air their grievances. Their Guaranteed Fair Treatment Policy (GFTP) is a process that gives employees the right to appeal any eligible issue through a systematic review by progressively higher levels of management. The GFTP process does not assure a judgment in their favor, but it does insure that employees can discuss complaints without fear of retaliation. FedEx, like other companies, also takes an annual anonymous survey of employee satisfaction with their management and company. FedEx then requires all managers to meet and discuss employee concerns within six weeks. If a manager's survey scores are low, then he or she is expected to develop and implement immediate corrections.

# MENTORING

Nurturing can be more than simply being receptive to employees' concerns. It can also involve professional development. One of FedEx's more unique nurturing programs is their mentoring program. It allows first-level managers with three years management experience to learn from other managers who are at the managing director level, their third level of management. Thus, a mentor is two levels above a manager. The purpose is to help guide and develop skills of those at the first two levels by putting people who want to succeed around those who have already succeeded. This is the essence of nurturing because it puts a more-skilled, experienced person with a less-skilled, less-experienced person. For two years the mentor and protégé will meet and with assistance from the human resources department draw up an agreement that describes the needs of the protégé and how the mentor will provide guidance.

Mentoring is not the only way this *people first* company is able to nurture and increase productivity. Thomas Westling is a manager of their aircraft line maintenance. He recently moved his ailing mother from Tampa to Memphis. The hard part was trying to find affordable housing, doctors, transferring benefits, and so on. He said, "I didn't know where to begin." He went to the library to get a list of government phone numbers. All that accomplished was to be bounced around and be put on hold. He finally got help from a most unexpected source—his company.

FedEx offers its employees an information and referral service it calls Life-Works to help their employees with problems of elderly parents. LifeWorks also helps employees with child care and education issues. Westling got a notice about LifeWorks so he called their toll-free number in Boston and was then directed to a counselor at Sevin Services, a nonprofit agency in Memphis. Through them, he was able to get a low-income housing referral list, a list of doctors, and information about Social Security and food stamps.

LifeWorks programs normally cost companies between $15 to $25 per employee but FedEx seems pleased with its investment. Kay Carter, senior manager in employee benefits services at FedEx, says that if it is good for employees, it's good for the company. Surveys of employees show that, when employees were trying to find housing for an elderly parent or deal with Social Security, the service saved six to ten hours a week. Mary Kay Leonard, vice president of Work-Family Directions, says the time saved is frequently work time and that is a straight productivity gain. She says if an employee is worried about his mother, then he probably is bringing the worry and anxiety to his job and that could result in diminished work performance (Campbell 1995).

# SUMMARY

A good example of having a willingness to experiment in the marketplace is provided by Sony. It is Sony's policy to send more products into the marketplace knowing that not all will be winners. Brian Bakoglu, senior vice president at Sony R-and-D labs in San Jose, says, "Sometimes it's much more comfortable to select two or three products you are 100 percent sure of, but you kill some innovative products that you may not be sure the market will accept." He goes on to say, "if you don't take risks, you will never know" (Stevens 1996).

It may be a hard and cold world out there, but executives who simply want to tell us the "facts of life" and expect us to adapt or die make a serious mistake. Winning requires that we take risks and strive to compete, and we do that when we feel we are not alone. Our need for nurturing is biological, and it is not enough to expect people to get it at home. Organizations like FedEx show that nurturing pays big and long-term dividends. Fear works too, but eventually it catches up with those who give us a stern eye and say adapt or die. Such philosophies may keep people in line and may make them obedient, but we need their creative hearts and minds. Everyone has creative potential, but it takes the right environment to bring it forth. Trying something new is a risk; it creates fear in a species that prefers the status quo. It is hard to be a radical and a risk taker if you think your next meal will be your last. Risk taking is an essential part of creativity and nurturing is an essential part of risk taking.

# REFERENCES

Amabile, Teresa M. 1996. Assessing the work environment for creativity. *Academy of Management Journal* 39, no. 5 (October): 59.

Caine, Renate Nummela, and Geoffrey Caine. 1994. *Making connections.* New York: Addison-Wesley, 69–70.

Campbell, Laurel. 1995. More local companies aiding employees in care for the elderly. *The Commercial Appeal Newspaper,* 29 January, C3.

Caulkin, Simon. 1995. Chaos Inc. *Across the Board* (July/August): 35.

Coyne, William E. 1996. Building a tradition of innovation, *U.K. Innovation Lecture,* 5 May: 9, 10.

Eisner, Michael. 1996. Speech to Chicago Executives Club. Chicago, 19 April, 4–7.

Freiberg, Kevin, and Jackie Freiberg. 1996. *Nuts! Southwest Airlines' crazy recipe for business and personal success.* Austin, Tex.: Bard Press, Inc., 60.

Grove, Andrew S. 1995. A high-tech CEO updates his views on managing and careers. *Fortune* 132, no. 6 (18 September): 229.

Henkoff, Ronald. 1993. Companies that train best. *Fortune,* (22 March): 62.

Kelly, Kevin. 1994. *Out of control.* Addison-Wesley Publishing Company.

Nemeth, Charlan Jeanne. 1997. Managing innovation: When less is more (creativity in management). *California Management Review* 40, no. 1 (fall): 67.

Order from chaos. 1994. *Management Today.*

Perry, Lee Tom. 1995. *Offensive strategy.* New York: Harper Business, 38–39.

Porter, Michael E. 1990. *The competitive advantage of nations.* New York: The Free Press.

Reed, David M. 1991. New product planning: Lesson from Japanese experience. *Journal of Marketing Management* 11: 355–69.

Silver, William S., and Terence R. Mitchell. 1990. The status quo tendency in decision making. *Organizational Dynamics* 18, no. 4 (spring): 37–45.

Stevens, Tim. 1996. Converting ideas into profits. *Industry Week* 245, no. 11 (3 June): 21.

Welsh, John F. 1993. A master class in radical change. *Fortune* 128, no. 15 (13 December): 83.

# CHAPTER 9

# Developing a Creative Workplace: Managing the Direction—Not the Details

## INTRODUCTION

Creativity and bureaucracy are not complementary concepts. Rigid control and order destroy the flexibility needed for innovative thinking. But some control must exist, otherwise anarchy and chaos might win the day. A creative workplace flourishes under spontaneous order. Bottom-up rules rather than top-down ones are needed. The trick is to create a flexible control based on gaining agreement over a few simple rules of behavior that encourage learning, adapting, improving, and cooperating. Creativity originates from simplicity, not complexity. The keys are to do the following:

- Identify your focal point
- Continue to clarify it
- Identify who you are through future scenarios
- Manage by applying broad, basic rules

Gifford Pinchot's book, *The End of Bureaucracy and the Rise of the Intelligent Organization,* discusses the need to go beyond conventional thinking about empowerment. He notes that a national economy run by government bureaucracy is not a system run by a better bureaucracy. A corporate bureaucracy is not merely training managers to behave in an empowered way within a bureaucracy structure. It is developing a system of freedoms and institutions analogous to free enterprise, what he calls free intraprise. It was meant to describe organizations in which innovation was encouraged (Pickard 1996).

Southwest Airlines is one organization that understands the risk of bureaucracy and rules. They believe bureaucracy creates dependency that makes people do what they are told and no more. CEO Kelleher says that their leanness (lack of bureaucracy and rules) requires people to be comfortable in making their own decisions and understanding their own efforts (Freiberg and Freiberg 1996, 76). Rules, like so many other bureaucratic actions, adversely affect creativity. Enron's President Richard Kinder best expressed the tentative nature of creativity when he said, "a good idea is fragile like a lighted match, easily blown out by the cold winds of rigid management" (O'Reilly 1997). The message is that if you want innovation and change, then you must get rid of as much bureaucracy as possible. Organizations need some stability and procedures that organize basic activities, but too many rules stifle creativity. All too often great ideas require multiple sign-offs and elaborate review processes. Important ideas that might help you to gain a competitive advantage are given as much attention as lesser ideas. There are historical lessons about the effects of such bureaucracy.

In the economy of Lenin's Russia, resources were allocated from the top by senior officials who identified tradeoffs and controlled those resources. Chaos theory tells us the folly of trying to have this much control. It was as unsuccessful as many current engineering efforts are at continually chasing down failures in the hope of bringing complete control over their projects. Frederick Hayek and other Austrian economists in the 1920s argued for controlling a single variable—the price—that is used to regulate all other variables (Kelly 1995, 121). This way you do not have to know how many bars of soap are needed by a person. It is control from the bottom up not, as in Lenin's case, top down. There is the *spontaneous order* rather than rigid order that must exist in the most creative workplaces.

Chaos theory shows us that the outcomes of changing a complex system, like organizations, can never be entirely predicted but it is possible to place your bets on the changes with the greatest odds of having a significant impact. Sometimes these key variables may be cost or competitors' moves or even customers' needs and desires. Those variables (money, customers, and so on) also can vary from one organization to another. First, identify those key variables affecting your business's survival, then identify key changes that are needed within your organization. For instance, if your market or customers are very stable, you may choose to improve efficiency rather than concentrate on increased expenditures on new product and development. On the other hand, if your product or service is in a period of decline, then it is time to explore potential in a newer product or service niche.

## BOTTOM-UP RULES

John H. Holland of the University of Michigan wonders how complex things change and adapt to their environments. The chaos theory and the science of complexity showed us that a few simple laws produce an enormously rich behavior of the world (Waldrop 1992, 153). It is similar to chess, which has a few number of rules but produces a game that is never the same twice. Originality, innovation, and creativity can come from simple rules.

Murray-Gell Mann in his book, *The Quark and the Jaguar,* points out that all complex systems acquire information about its environment and its adaptation to it (for example, where we are, how are we doing). These systems try to identify regularities in the information and then try to condense those regularities into a kind of *schema* (Mann 1994, 17) or model. There is Darwinian selective pressure among these operational models. Some are demoted in a hierarchy or eliminated altogether if they do not help predict future actions. This method provides a simplified but effective way of interacting with and understanding its environment. Even very complex undertakings can be managed through simplified control.

NASA, like normal organizations, must also deal with the issue of control. Long distances in planetary exploration make the need for rapid feedback of utmost importance. Engineers at the Jet Propulsion Laboratory are creating micro-rovers that will act more like ants than anything else. They are self-powered, self-guided, and, once released, are out of control in the sense that they do not need constant supervision. They can be programmed with simple rules or so-called "bottom-up" control. If you break off one of the robot's legs, it will shift gaits to the others that are left so it can maintain its gait. Their rules are simple such as, "If I feel something, I'll stop; if I don't, I keep going." Other rules deal with overcoming obstacles. Rodney Brooks, a MIT professor, describes some of his bottom-up rules for his robots. They provide a hierarchy of rules from bottom up including: (1) avoid contact with objects; (2) wander aimlessly; (3) explore the world; (4) build an internal map; (5) notice changes in the environment; and (6) formulate travel plans and anticipate and modify plans accordingly (Kelly 1995, 38–40).

## TO ENCOURAGE INNOVATION, DEVELOP BROAD BASIC RULES

The behaviors involve adding new behaviors to older ones from the bottom up. Control is accumulated by incremental additions. Broader basic rules, like avoid contact, are not messed with but rather additional higher level rules are added but never altered. For instance, if a lower rule, like wander aimlessly, gets in the way of a higher rule or behavior, it is suppressed—not eliminated. Broad bottom rules are never ignored, just suppressed (Kelly 1995, 40).

Control in creative organizations begins with simple behaviors, ones that are almost instinctive or reflexive. You create a simple rule that handles simple jobs. You use many of these simple rules. Then you overlap these simple rules with a secondary level of rules for more complex behavior. Brooks recommends that complex behavior follows a certain process including the following:

1. Do simple things first.
2. Learn to do them flawlessly.
3. Add new layers of activity over the results of these simple tasks.
4. Do not change the simple things.
5. Make the new layer work as flawlessly as the simple one.
6. Repeat, ad infinitum (Kelly 1995, 41).

All this focus on rules may not seem very different than centralized and bureaucratic thinking associated with rigid order, but nothing could be further from the truth. Most organizational leaders faced with a complex task too often come up with a list of all the tasks needing to be done, determine the order they are to be done, and then direct completion from central command. The best example of this approach is that of the former Soviet Union. Such a system collapses, not because of the rules, but because of control from the top. Everything designed around a central command cannot be flexible and innovative. With the right rules, you can build a direction and a mind, without a mind. **The right rules are those aimed at learning, adapting, improving, cooperating, and competing.** Otherwise, you have static bureaucracy that is concerned with maintaining the status quo. Creativity comes from simple rules arranged in hierarchy. The key point is that innovative work areas require that information and authority come from the bottom up and side to side, not from the top down.

## RULES THAT ENCOURAGE CREATIVITY

Simplicity, not complexity, is the centerpiece of creative organizations. Chaos theory teaches us that simplicity in design can produce complex reactions through sheer multiplication of possibilities. A good example of how this occurs comes from a computer program called *Boids*.

Craig Reynolds of the Symbolics Corporation in Los Angeles created simulation in which he placed a large collection of autonomous, bird like agents called *boids* into a computer screen full of walls and obstacles. Each boid was programmed with only three simple rules of behavior.

1. Maintain a minimum distance from other objects in the environment, including other boids (translation: don't crash into each other)

2. Try to match the velocities with boids in its neighborhood (translation: fly at the same speed)

3. Try to move toward the perceived center of a mass of boids in its neighborhood (translation: reduce your drag)

None of these rules said form a flock or react in creative ways, but the boids did. The rules only referred to what an individual boid could see and do in its own vicinity. If a flock was going to occur, it would have to occur from the ground up rather than being directed by some central authority. Flocks did form into the familiar *V* shape that geese and other birds assume. Each boid acted selfishly, but was driven to work together through a *common purpose.* They would spontaneously collect themselves into a flock that could fly around obstacles in a natural and fluid way. Sometimes the flock would even break into subflocks that flowed around both sides of an obstacle, then rejoin on the other side, just as if it had been planned. In one run, a boid accidentally hit a pole, it fluttered around for a moment as though stunned and lost, then darted forward to join the flock as it moved on (Waldrop 1992, 242).

Flocking was also demonstrated in the movie *Batman Returns* which shows a large mass of black bats swarming through tunnels. Those bats were computer generated by first creating a single bat that was  given leeway to flap its wings. The bat was copied until they had a mob. Then each bat was given computer instructions to do the following: (1) don't bump into another bat; (2) keep up with your neighbors; and (3) don't stray too far away. When the program was run, they flocked like real bats (Kelly 1995, 10–11).

---

## CREATE A COMMON FOCAL POINT

---

A great deal of innovation and creativity could occur if we simulated these computer programs by developing a common focus for our people. These common organizational focal points would dictate that they (1) don't crash into each other (we're a team); (2) keep up with the rest of us; and (3) go to the same place. Creativity demands that we have a set of a few simple controls, rather than detailed ones, to guide complex reactions for changing environmental conditions. Creative acts do not require complex organizational structures, in fact they impede innovation.

Creativity comes easiest when the business environment is brought down to its simplest component, its focal points. This can be done by concentrating on at least three coordinates. The first of these, like the computer program, is to **know your identity**. In Boids, the dots were told to act like birds by reducing their drag. In organizations, it is essential to determine how to work together. To do that, we need to know "who and where we are at." This does not mean describing what a department or function does or providing a job description. Rather it entails arriving at a strong consensus about the parameters of our culture and then clarifying what we are trying to accomplish.

# A CLEAR IDENTITY

In Collins and Porros's book, *Built to Last,* the authors attempted to analyze visionary companies that were nominated by CEOs as being good, successful, and enduring. Enduring meant founded before 1950 with multiple product or service life cycles. Examples included Hewlett-Packard, IBM, Procter and Gamble, Wal-Mart, GE, Boeing, 3M, Nordstrom, Merck, and Walt Disney. Collins and Porros's analysis of these successful and less successful ones showed one particular characteristic that trademarked successful ones. The authors say these visionary companies are marked by a cultlike atmosphere, which includes fervently held ideology, indoctrination, and a high degree of *fit* or uniformity. Such comparisons between a strong culture and cults have been noted by other authors (Nemeth 1997). Strong cultures leave little doubt about "who we are." A narrow range of perspective is essential for uniform actions among diverse members of a group.

Defining who we are begins with an employee initial indoctrination and continues throughout their service. It must be comprehensive emersion, but it need not be complex. Nordstrom's employee handbook consists of a single 5″ × 8″ card with the rule: "Use your good judgment in all situations. There will be no additional rules" (Nemeth 1997, 61). The standard operating procedures may be simple, but job socialization, guidance, mentoring, approval and disapproval by peers, and storytelling—as well as continual ranking and feedback—make the emersion complete. Such a culture is an organization's memory that guides behavior and gives everyone a sense of identity, stability, and boundary (Freiberg and Freiberg 1996, 145). Authors Kevin and Jackie Freiberg believe Southwest Airlines has a thick culture. This almost seamless fabric is one where the threads (for example, values, philosophies, and norms of behavior) are difficult to isolate.

Southwest only has a few standing committees—one of which is a culture committee. They are in large part a committee of a hundred storytellers made up of flight attendants, reservationists, and others, including top executives. The committee of organizational storytellers works behind the scenes to foster their cultural identity (Freiberg and Freiberg 1996, 165). The committee has four all-day meetings each year and several ad hoc committees are formed more frequently throughout the year. Committee members have been seen with paint in hand, remodeling a break room, or appearing with pizza and ice cream to serve the maintenance workers. Culture is also enhanced at Southwest through their day-in-the-field experience. Personnel throughout the year help do another's job and often share the experience in their in-house communication newsletter, *LUV Lines*.

Creating a *thick* culture or cultlike atmosphere like Southwest's is driven by many psychological forces. Peer pressure is a factor. When people are faced with a majority of others who agree or an attitude or judgment, they are very likely to adopt that majority judgment. Basically, people believe that there is truth in numbers, plus many fear disapproval and rejection for being different. The fear of being different and the need to be accepted and avoid ridicule or rejection are forces that drive people's behavior toward a central focus. Most will seek to corroborate the majority position. Obviously, too much of this can prove a disadvantage when seeking novel or original insights, but it does tend to focus people in a common direction.

## DEFINING WHO WE ARE

A definition of who you are should not be too vague because people will not know what to do and will feel they are out of control. Predictability and order are an essential need of all people. Likewise, we do not need too detailed explanations of who we are because it will destroy our creativity and innovation. For instance, suppose a definition of "we sell shoes" and that "customer satisfaction is our most important objective." This may be what is said, but the reality is often far different. Sometimes there are hidden agendas; people can seek to selfishly put themselves in a better position regardless of others. Many end up developing their own unique perspectives about what is involved in selling shoes or satisfying the customer. We do not "act like birds," but rather like individual dots that randomly drift from left to right and up to down.

---

CONTINUALLY CLARIFY YOUR FOCUS

---

Knowing who and what we are cannot be a vague idea (sell shoes, drive a truck, or program a computer). Everyone within the organization must be absolutely clear about the simple but specific rules that are the centerpiece of all actions. It must be a "cultural thing," created by strong gene or information flow. Creativity demands that people within the organization must understand what to do when conditions change. This does not require a set of detailed standard operational procedures or detailed strategic planning, but rather a set of moral or religious guides to behavior.

Southwest's CEO Herb Kelleher puts little stock in strategic planning. He believes that writing something down in a plan makes it gospel; and when a plan becomes gospel, it becomes easy for people to become too rigid in their thinking (Freiberg and Freiberg 1996). His point is that, "Reality is chaotic; planning is ordered and logical," so you have to have a direction, but you must also be flexible and reactive.

If you are to act like a bird, a shoe salesperson, a truck driver, or a computer programmer, what are you trying to accomplish? Birds try to stay in the air, shoe salespeople and truck drivers may be told to satisfy the customer or make money, but there is a difference. Birds *intuitively* know what is needed to keep them up there. Salespeople, truck drivers, or computer programmers rarely know how to get up there or where they are headed. They may be told what to do but are not told how to evaluate decisions.

If customer satisfaction is really the objective, and everyone really does know their job, then we should not need someone telling us how to do it. Specific, detailed instructions do the same thing, but they destroy creativity and innovation. Southwest uses future scenario generation rather than strategic planning as a way of preparing for the future. This *what if* game is played by the company's executive planning committee. They meet periodically to create future scenarios in which the organization could find itself. Sessions include many *what if* questions designed to get the group thinking about possible situations the company could face. Questions like "what if we do . . . , then how will the competition respond?" or "what if our competition provides a new service that . . . , then what would we do?" The outcome of the scenario discussion is a set of multiple plans that helps them to keep focused on a common direction—on who they are and where they want to go.

When you know who you are and where you are going, you are able to exercise good judgment and do the right thing even where it seems to conflict with the normal standard operating procedures. It is when your principles are fuzzy that you get rule-bound, bureaucratic thinking.

Rod Jones, an assistant chief pilot at Southwest, tells of a captain who left the gate with a senior citizen who had boarded the wrong plane. The customer was very confused and upset. Southwest pilots are asked not to go back to the gate with an incorrectly boarded customer, but the captain was concerned about the well-being of the individual. So he broke the rule and came back to the gate, deplaned the customer, pushed back out, and filled out an irregularity report. Southwest's response was "Attaboy" (Freiberg and Freiberg 1996, 88).

Creativity demands that we let our people specifically know what customers expect and leave it up to them to figure out how best to satisfy them. If we really do not know what customers want or how to make money, or how to provide quality service, then it is a deeper problem. In this case, it is not so much a matter of clarifying who we are, it is a case of not really *knowing* where you are at.

It is only when we know what customers want or how to make money (or whatever your focal point is) and where we are in satisfying those goals that creativity, not control, can grow. If we have intelligent people, then we should get a pretty good decision from them. It may not have been the exact decision a manager would have made, but it will be an equally good one. This, again, all assumes we have a deep understanding about our customers, profits, quality, or other focal point.

Innovation and creativity demands that we do not micromanage the details. Rather we continually reinforce who we are, where we're headed, how we are doing, and teach people *why* they are important. Creative organizations spend far less time teaching people how to be good truck drivers or shoe salespeople and less time controlling the details. Far greater time is spent clarifying what they are trying to do for their customers than inspiring people and showing them what it takes to satisfy customers, control costs, or whatever else is essential to survival. Leaders in such organizations will spend most of their time discovering what is needed and the rest of the time as teachers, explaining what they have discovered. So what happens to supervision? How do we insure what we know is converted into action?

# CONTROL AND CREATIVITY

Creating an abundance of top-down rules, goals, objectives, and strategies is a useful Confucianism strategy for organizations that function in a very stable work environment, one that is below the zone of creativity. Rigid controls do work reasonably well provided your competition, cost, customers, or outside environmental forces do not significantly change. Leaders in a more dynamic environment, though, recognize that you can only control the past, the future is in a constant state of flux. If you need creativity, speed, and greater competitiveness, then avoid getting distracted by the details. Rather keep people focused on your common focal point about who you are, where you are at, and then provide good feedback on how things are changing.

---

### PROVIDE CONTINUAL FEEDBACK ON PERFORMANCE

---

The Springfield Remanufacturing Company (SRC) is an employee owned and operated company that rebuilds diesel and gasoline engines. The thing that makes them special is not their work but how they keep everyone focused on their common focal point (to generate wealth). SRC teaches their people where they are at by teaching them how to read and understand their weekly income statements and balance sheets so they know how things are changing. On a weekly basis, everyone, including their janitors (some say a somewhat lowly bird), knows individually how they contribute to their bottom line. They do this by continually comparing positive and negative variations from line items on the income statements (where we are at).

SRC is different from most companies. No end-of-the-quarter recognition, no annual performance appraisal—by that time, we would already have crashed into each other, drifted off course, or fallen behind. They need weekly, even daily, or ideally even hourly feedback about those conditions essential to satisfy the customer, make money, and so on. The more closely we need to be coordinated to satisfy those objectives, the more frequently we need feedback. Organizations that focus on customer satisfaction, quality, or other objectives need similar coordinates to quantify and report everyone's (department's, function's, and individual's) current position relative to those objectives.

Three little rules—identify yourself (who are we), provide information about where you are at, and then create constant feedback about how you are doing—are the backbone of the creative workplace. Creative organizations' personnel require a great deal more information or coordinates about where they are than the typical organization, but the outcome can produce far more innovative shoe salespeople, truck drivers, bankers, and other personnel.

# SUMMARY

Typical leaders usually try to clarify their vision about what they would like the organization to be. In military fashion, they create a mission statement that identifies specific tasks to be carried out, then strategies are developed for achieving certain goals, objectives are clarified, goals defined, and rules established. Leaders interested in developing a creative workplace minimize the number of rules and regulations and only create *temporary* goals, objectives, strategies, and missions. The more dynamic the environment, the more likely each of these will need to be flexible. Defining (1) who we are, (2) where we are at, and (3) how we are doing should be the only things that have any resemblance to a sense of permanence.

Feedback on performance may mean achieving reasonable cost efficiencies, profits, and productivity, but your numbers should complement not distract from who you are. For instance, focusing on great customer service will require using measures that track it. A critical test will be to develop a link between customer service and improved financial results and efficiency. If you are not doing this, then you are not measuring the right things. Measuring results that contribute to increased financial results and improved productivity performance include things like loyalty or retention rates, increased business, or resistance to lowering prices (Steward 1995). Customer satisfaction measures should address at least some of these issues. Find out what keeps customers coming back and remaining loyal by asking them, then measure those results.

Bottom-up rules can be used once you have your focal point and have a strong sense of where you are at and how you are doing. Bottom-up rules allow a degree of control without the suffocating control usually associated with bureaucracy. An amazing degree of complexity can come from simple behaviors that are religiously adhered. It is not control from the top, but rather a system that slowly builds complex behaviors. Such rules focus on learning, adapting, cooperating, and competing. The boids simulation demonstrates how simple rules lead to complex, effective, and creative behavior.

# REFERENCES

Freiberg, Kevin, and Jackie Freiberg. 1996. *Nuts! Southwest Airlines' crazy recipe for business and personal success.* Austin, Tex.: Bard Press, Inc., 76.

Kelly, Kevin. 1995. *Out of control.* Boston, Mass.: Addison-Wesley.

Mann, Murray-Gell. 1994. *The quark and the jaguar.* New York: W. H. Freeman and Company.

Nemeth, Charlan Jeanne, 1997. Managing innovation: When less is more (creativity in management). *California Management Review* 40, 1 (fall): 67.

O'Reilly, B. O. 1997. The secrets of America's most admired corporations: New ideas, new products. *Fortune* 135, no. 4 (3 March): 60–64.

Pickard, Jane. 1996. A fertile ground. *People Management* 2, no. 21 (24 October): 28–31.

Steward, T. A. 1993. Welcome to the revolution. *Fortune,* 13 December.

Waldrop, M. Mitchell. 1992. *Complexity: The emerging science at the edge of order and chaos.* New York: Simon & Schuster.

# CHAPTER 10

# Innovation through Technology:
# A Historical Lesson

## INTRODUCTION

Technological breakthroughs change the basis of competition. Historically, we know that every technology grows old and is replaced by newer ones. We also know this shift in technology often results in shifts in competitive advantage. Nature and the British can teach us much about what we should do to gain this competitive advantage. Some of these lessons include the following:

- Develop useful applications for useless by-products
- Invest in leapfrogging technology
- Implement **lumpy improvement,** rather than continuous improvement

A recent survey by the Product Development and Management Association indicated that more than 30 percent of survey respondents' annual sales come from products less than five years old. Furthermore, throughout all industries, the high-growth achievers and industry leaders said that their percentage was significantly higher than the 30 percent reaching up to 49 percent (Successful 1995). The message is that if you and I are competing and I can read the market quicker, bring out new products faster, make many different products on the same line, or instantly change over to other products or services, then I win. The ever-present need to innovate is a lesson we should have drawn from history.

What do barrelmakers, blacksmiths, and manufacturers of buggy-whips and slide rules have in common? Well, there are not many of them around any more. At one time, they were highly prized and were a source of many jobs. Those that found ways to make more efficient barrels or were more productive buggy-whip or slide rule makers enjoyed a higher standard of living. Surely there was concern for customer appeal for improving operations for dealing with their competitors' next move. Then it all changed, and they had simply outlived their usefulness.

# THE RED QUEEN

Great Britain, during Victorian times, was able to dominate the world because it was able to manufacture and use relevant tools and technology better than anyone on the face of the planet. But Great Britain should have listened to the Red Queen's advice in Lewis Carroll's *Through the Looking Glass* in which she says that to stay in place you have to run very, very hard and to get anywhere you have to run even harder. Victorian England forgot the Red Queen's wisdom and Britain lost her dominance of the world. Victorians said the sun never set on their empire. England did dominate 25 percent of the land surface. They ruled more than 20 million square miles of territory and a quarter of the globe's population (Tuchman 1979, 63) and they produced 27.9 percent of all the world's goods. Today the British share of world productivity has slipped to 3 percent (Kennedy 1987); so what happened?

From 1790 to 1815 British exports skyrocketed. They came up with startling technological innovations. Asians had already figured out how to turn a scrubby bush into cotton, but the British discovered how to produce it at bargain-basement prices. They also figured out how to mass-produce pig iron—a substance of worldwide demand. British ships controlled the sea lanes, and they developed markets for merchandise everywhere from India to South America.

From 1796 to 1812 France's Napoleon humbled nearly every nation he encountered—Spain, Holland, Prussia, Austria, Egypt—but somehow could not bring the pesky British (he called them a "nation of shopkeepers") to their knees. One of the main reasons was that England kept making profits and reinvesting them in industrial innovation and military resistance to Napoleon. Napoleon may have been a great general, but he was a lousy manager because he failed to understand the importance of industrial innovation. Management workers and bosses within his empire were mired in obsolete technologies and eventually he could not afford his armies. He overlooked the fact that military might depends not just on guns and strategic brilliance but on industrial innovation and marketing smarts. The next 59 years were good ones for Britain, in large part because of technological innovation.

The first of these technologies was the spread of mechanization (beyond the mere cotton mills) and the second was steam. The British mastered both, including how to use steam engines to make goods that artisans had taken great pain to produce by hand. One machine-operating British worker could turn out as much cloth as 20 old-fashioned competitors. In Queen Victoria's day (1837–1901), productivity per person in Britain rose 2.5 times! Wages rose an astonishing 80 percent in real dollars from 1850 to 1900. The world could not wait to get its hands on inexpensive, high-tech British goods. By 1860 the English—with 2 percent of the world's population—were turning out 25 percent of the world's wares and over 40 percent of the items from modern industrial plants. Transactions everywhere were financed by British banks and insured by British insurance companies.

They knew their prosperity depended on the fact that they were ahead of other countries in commercial utilization of technology and banned export of high-tech fabric-making machines—but they grew fat with prosperity. The power of the status quo began to grow. They forgot the following facts:

1. Every technological breakthrough grows old.

2. New inventions arrive to replace it.

3. Those that dominate these new technologies rule the world (Mass and Senge 1981).

Oddly, technologies that made steam look old-fashioned were developed in Britain, but self-satisfied British industrialists seldom tried to turn them into tempting new products.

## BY-PRODUCTS OF THE BRITISH COLLAPSE

British soldiers on Indian soil during this period had only half the life expectancy of compatriots back home. Malaria decimated British troops in India. Illness became a serious obstacle to British colonization. White men who traveled a few miles inland in Africa invariably became sick and died because of malaria. There was hope the innovative use of the bark of a Peruvian plant could be used to produce a compound called quinine. However, British botanists had almost no luck in cultivating enough of the plants to make even the smallest amount of quinine.

The driving force for R and D during this time was to find a solution to the quinine problem. It was the competitive advantage essential to British success. Concurrently, during this time the British also learned how to extract a vapor from coal and use this gas for lighting, but the process produced a useless by-product—coal tar. Disposing of the useless stuff was a messy business. At London's Royal College of Chemistry, a German professor suggested to an assistant that he see if he could somehow create artificial quinine from the goo. The assistant, William Perkin, tried but failed. Instead of quinine, he ended up with a liquid whose color was the shade of mauve. When he tried the solution as a cloth dye, it worked! He realized he had something special so he dropped his assistantship, borrowed money from his father, and opened up a small factory outside London. Before long, even Queen Victoria was wearing gowns tinted with Perkin's mauve.

> ### FIND USES FOR IRRELEVANT INNOVATIONS

Despite Perkin's rapid rise to millionaire status, most British industrialists ignored his discovery—that is, everyone except the Germans. They worked to find out what other innovative by-products they could extract from coal tar. In 1863 one German researcher came up with what chaos theorists would cite as an example of small changes having a disproportional large consequence. It was a rich shade of green. When Empress Eugenie wore this color to the Paris Opera, it became the fashion rage. Demand drove experiments—by the Germans, not the British.

After Perkin retired at age 36, the British dye industry faded in his absence but the German dye business began the first step in a revolutionary technology. Their experiments with coal dye became the foundation of their chemical industry (Burke 1978). The exploration of this seemingly irrelevant by-product would have far-flung implications for both nations. One example of a useful by-product of the initial coal tar by-product was the use of chemical fertilizers with which German farmers soon were able to produce more food per acre than any other nation. England invented, then discarded, a seemingly useless process. Germany used the British by-product to gain in competitive strength.

# RUN—VERY, VERY HARD

English steam engines would soon begin to look old-fashioned. The greatest physicists of the age—Britishers Michael Faraday and James Clerk Maxwell—were experimenting with electricity but British industrialists did not look at what practical uses they could find for the pair's discoveries. Those who did were Americans and Germans. Britain's Faraday had earlier discovered the principle of an alternating-current transformer but had not bothered to pursue the technological implications. The first electric-generating plant in Britain to sell power to the ordinary householder was built by Thomas Edison.

In 1873 Britain went through a Great Depression that lasted for 20 years. Steam technology was on the decline. Other countries were producing inexpensive fabrics. There was a demand for new products, those being produced by Germany's chemical industry and electrical devices, with great consumer appeal were made by Americans and Germans.

German exports tripled from 1890 to 1913. By 1913 German companies Sieman and AEG dominated the European electrical industry. German chemical giants Bayer and Hoechst would produce 90 percent of the world's industrial dyes. On the American side, Andrew Carnegie in 1902 produced more steel than all the factories of England combined.

Competitiveness comes from cultivating innovative minds. Germany maintained the best school system, and by the 1890s had 2.5 times as many university students per unit of population as England. Germany was on the move and eventually it would lead to World War I. Britain won, but lost her prosperity. The British worker became the lowest, not the highest, paid. Her factories became the most inefficient when they used to be the most efficient.

The lesson seems clear. Success depends on finding and converting new innovations into producible goods. There is a need to aggressively develop useful applications from what many would consider useless by-products. The focus should be on innovation not on the narrower process of improving a process or technology. Ask "what do we do with this?" Every irrelevant change can and often does produce new winners and losers. To stay in place, you have to run. To get anywhere, you have to run very, very hard!

Investment in change, not in a particular technology, is the key to successful technological innovation. A 1995 product development benchmarking study by the management consulting firm, Pittiglio Rabin Todd and McGrath, used a R and D effectiveness index to determine an industry's overall effectiveness. They found that return on R-and-D investment had increased 84 percent since 1992. Their index tracks the level of R-and-D spending, as well as profit for every dollar of product development investment. In 1992 companies received a return of 25 cents in new products. In 1993 it rose to 31 cents and, in 1994, to 46 cents. In 1994 the United States spent $100 billion—that translates to a $21 billion improvement since 1992 (High-tech 1995). Innovation, and particularly R and D, pays; but it is not so much about the money spent as it is about how it's spent.

## NATURE'S LESSONS ABOUT TECHNOLOGY'S EVOLUTION

The earliest signs of life go back 3.45 billion years ago. By 800 million years ago, multicellular organisms appeared. Then something truly remarkable occurred. About 550 million years ago the Cambrian explosion occurred. It is called the explosion because there was not a process on continual or gradual improvement, but rather a sudden and dramatic reengineering occurred. It was during this time that almost all the major divisions of plants and animals suddenly appeared. Only the vertebrates, which is our own niche, arose later. For the next 100 million years, things happened which seem to challenge common sense.

When we look at organisms, humans tend to group them hierarchically from specific to general. The Linnean chart does this and goes from species (which are capable of breeding with each other) to genera (groups of several species) to families of these species to still larger orders and classes and to still larger phyla and finally to kingdoms. Logic would lead us to believe therefore that the first multicellular creatures would be very similar. Only later would we expect them to diversify from the bottom up. First we might expect to see one species, then see related groups of species or genera, and then see these evolve to eventually still broader groups of families and so on. Darwin would have thought this because he proposed that all evolution occurred by very gradual accumulations of useful adaptations and variations. Using this logic, early multicellular creatures should have diverged gradually from one another, but this did not happen. It seems that in the Cambrian explosion, our chart filled in from the top down, not the bottom up! There was a sudden explosion of widely different and innovative biological body plans. It was the broader phyla, not the more closely related species, that came first. There were sudden, unexpected, and quite original innovations rather than enhancements of current products. This Cambrian explosion is not what we normally expect, but that is exactly what happened.

## CAMBRIAN PATTERNS

Technological innovation, like the Cambrian explosion, also seems to fill in from the top. Striking variations arise early and then diminish to minor or continual improvements. Each major innovation can be greatly improved upon by making design variations. Later on, when most of the variations have been explored, nature and human product and service designers begin worrying about the details. Specialization and extinction of biological and technological life go together. For 100 million years, in the Cambrian period, diversity increased to a point where a steady state existed. Nature's approach to her own innovation is an approach that can work for organizations. 3M takes much the same Cambrian approach when they begin talking about their own technological innovation.

## INVEST IN LEAPFROGGING TECHNOLOGY

As Chairman and CEO of 3M L. D. DeSimone puts it—innovation is the engine of growth (Coyne 1996). This is evident by 3M's growth. During 1995, revenues for 3M's operations increased by $1.3 billion. The products they launched in 1995 generated revenues of $850 million. So two-thirds of their growth came from products introduced in 1995.

William E. Coyne, Senior Vice President of Research and Development at present-day 3M, says they pursue many projects at once, but place their biggest bets on products that *change the basis of competition*. They want products and services that redefine what is expected by the customer. They want to leapfrog the competition. For instance, silk-screening has been the historical standard for creating a high-quality image. It is expensive if you want to produce only a few signs, or mark a few vehicles. 3M developed an electrostatic printer system that can make durable, photographic quality, wall-and-truck-sized graphics. They do this at a price that allows customers to make a few or even one image (Coyne 1996). Another example of their competition-changing products is the 3M™ Dry View™ Laser Imaging System. It allows radiologists to develop high-quality, hard-copy images from CT scanners and magnetic resonance imagers. Its quality is good, but what really changes the basis of competition is that it produces the image without the plumbing, maintenance, fumes, and disposal cost of traditional wet-chemistry development technology. It seems that 3M has learned a thing or two. The same message can be seen from our world's earliest days.

Developing major, competitive changing, technological innovation like those of 3M is similar to the branching radiations of the Cambrian explosion. Soon after multicelled creatures were invented, many fundamentally different life forms suddenly appeared. Major innovations in body plans were followed by gradually finer and finer adjustments. Some innovations drive others extinct; that is what 3M is trying to do. The marketplace changes the landscape we all live on and creates selective pressures for some technology and not for others. Radically new technological innovations are rapidly followed by dramatic improvements and then gradual improvements in the technology. The bicycle, when invented, had little wheels, then big wheels, two seats, and so forth. Extinction followed and only the most fit design prevailed. Stuart Kauffman notes that it seems to be a natural law that after increasingly long periods of no improvement, sudden improvements often occur. These improvements then typically reach a plateau and all improvement ceases (Kauffman 1995, 204). Aggressive organizations, like 3M, would seem to stack the deck in their favor of developing *basis changing* innovation if they were to focus on areas where little or no incremental innovation seems to be occurring. The Cambrian pattern shows that the amount of cost reduction or innovation achieved with each improvement in a technology slows exponentially while the rate of finding such improvements also slows exponentially.

# USING CAMBRIAN LOGIC

Recent research has found some striking similarities between nature's lumpy approach to innovations and the most successful organizations' research and development tactics. In general, it appears that the introduction of a new technology does trigger an initial burst of creative activity as users explore the new technology and fix unexpected problems (Tyre and Orlikowski 1993, 13). This initial burst of activity is often followed by a dramatic decline within the first few months.

Researchers Tyre and Orlikowski looked at several manufacturers and service organizations in the United States and Europe. They studied 41 projects involving the introduction of new technology. The initial burst of activity was shortly thereafter followed by a rapid fall off of activity and effort. An important point to recognize is that experimenting and creative use of the technology is more likely to occur *immediately* following the technology's introduction rather than later. The rapid fall off occurred even though outstanding problems had not been addressed or resolved!

The initial period of introduction of new technology was not the only period that learning occurred. These new technological introductions often started new bursts of activity. These events were short-lived but did help users gain new insights. This cycle of intensive improvement and innovations in the technology followed by relatively stable operations is very much a Cambrian fingerprint. It is also the pattern that repeated itself over and over in Tyre and Orlikowski's research. They found on average that 54 percent of all activity dealing with the new technology occurred in the first three months in only 12 percent of the average total time for full integration of the technology. The pattern was consistent, regardless of size. This pattern *did not* exist simply because the users had resolved all the problems within that period. In fact, most of the new technologies would not be considered production worthy for several more months.

# IMPLEMENT LUMPY CHANGE

This does not mean that all problems after this period were ignored. After the initial explosion of activity, technologies enter a phase of regular use. Some time later, usually after many months, people would regroup and refocus attention on modifications—again in a concentrated manner. This discontinuous pattern did not seem to be a conscious management policy in any of the companies studied. Rather managers within the organization would often state that they recognized the need for continuous improvement to technologies but that it was difficult to keep people focused on this sort of activity. Familiarity often led to users simply taking it for granted. They naturally sought a level of status quo and stability.

However, disruptions did occur, which occasionally forced users to ask new questions and reexamine old problems. These disruptions were usually new developments that somehow disrupted routine operations like events that suddenly placed new demands on existing operations. For example, when new machines were added, it increased demand and temporarily shut down the line. The introduction of new products, product requirements, or new production procedures—as well as occasional breakdowns—were also times when the need for improvement became more apparent.

This noncontinuous pattern of technological improvements is very similar to biologists' punctuated equilibrium. Initial explosion of activity, followed by longer periods of relatively routine operation, is the norm. This initial explosion is often followed sometime later by another explosion caused by some unusual event.

# DOWN WITH THE CONTINUAL IMPROVEMENT!

Researchers Tyre and Orlikowski discovered that successful Japanese operations do not expect continuous improvements to new technologies. Managers in these organizations both create and exploit these punctuated equilibrium patterns by first aggressively using the introduction to adapt new technologies. They do this by identifying and making the maximum number of modifications as early as possible. Next, they impose routine use of the technology and use the time to teach use of the technology. Finally, they periodically create new opportunities for further adaptation (Tyre and Orlikowski 1993, 17).

The point is that they do not build much extra time in for debugging a new technology before moving into production. Using an adaptive challenge strategy, they put intentional stress on their system by developing very demanding early production commitments. Then they take steps to insure that the new technology will be ready. This requires intense revision early on rather than a continual stream of engineering changes. The Japanese firms still had problems to deal with but had to resolve them in the brief start-up period. Along with this compressed start-up is a significant commitment of resources. For instance, Toyota's design engineers, manufacturing engineers, production control, and quality managers live on the production floor during start-ups. Engineering changes are made on the spot (Tyre and Orlikowski 1993, 17).

This is not to say that the Japanese do not continually pursue improvement, because they do. However, this improvement does not occur in a constant stream of changes, rather it is more of a punctuated equilibrium. Except for urgent corrections, these Japanese managers are permitted to make changes to technology or production practices only at designated times (Hall 1983; Schonberger 1982).

Studies show a naturally lumpy pattern of technological innovation. Effective managers exploit it by carefully managing these spurts. This discontinuous pattern is a good fit for the natural surge of energy that normally occurs at the start of a project. This is followed by a period of routine operation that can be used for enhancing learning. The initial introduction of new technology is a special opportunity for management.

Energy levels are high, which makes this time the best one for influencing the effectiveness of the technology. The motivation to change is at the highest at the beginning and soon fades over time. Therefore, modification and changes in the technology is easiest at the beginning of the projects. There is one simple reason for taking advantage of this initial burst of activity. At the beginning, there are fewer competing demands on people's times. In his study of Toyota, Hall argues that a constant stream of changes can seriously compromise effectiveness (Hall 1983, 200).

Psychologists also note the people's motivation to solve problems is partly a function of time. The more exposure to a problem the less alert and fewer details they notice (Newtson 1973). It seems that familiarity makes people less willing to take the time and effort for difficult problem solving (Langer and Imber 1979).

After the initial introduction of the technology, there are good reasons to continue short but intensive spurts rather than to use a more gradual pattern of change. Many of the problems that affect the introduction of new technology require divergent perspectives of managers, engineers, and operational personnel. Gathering the resources once to attack a problem is more efficient than repeatedly getting them together. Continuing this program of short spurts of change and longer periods of regular use helps to focus people's attention after they have had time to gain experience with it.

## CREATING CAMBRIAN OPPORTUNITIES

Recognizing these initial patterns would suggest that managers begin to consider how to create opportunities for the burst of activities. Attention should be paid to how to use those opportunities as well as how to make the best use of regular flatter periods. Creating new opportunities could occur through adaptive challenges through occasional audits of how the technology is doing. Using a stretch goal approach that pushes the system to the limit might also be another approach. Setting extremely high standards for a short period might also force intensive problem solving.

An opposite but potentially effective approach is a sudden injection of new resources for only a short period of time. This could be a special day during which all attention is turned to solving key problems, upgrading equipment, or undertaking a new refinement. There are potentially many approaches but the key is to react rapidly during a limited time. Tight time limits help groups to concentrate and develop new innovations. However, it is essential that these deadlines do not become unrealistic or so rigid that they become dysfunctional. It should also be understood that new opportunities can be created in the future. This second change approach may also help managers set more realistic expectations and deadlines.

# SUMMARY

Stephan Jay Gould has observed, "wind back the tape of life to the dawn of time, let it play again, and you will never get humans a second time, nor the dinosaurs" (Lesson 1992). We humans, and all our artifacts, are here by the slimmest of chances. Extinction, not life, is the iron rule of biology.

Lessons from the British experience are worth noting. Being the best is never insurance against extinction. The world of change is not a rational model. It is your continual willingness to change rather than commitment to a particular technology that is essential. Sticking with what made you successful can be a serious mistake; even depending on superior technology is a risky proposition. The status quo in all forms is a powerful force, one that can ultimately bring down nations and organizations.

Individuals, groups, organizations, products, processes, services, and nations go extinct almost on a daily basis. The history of earth records at least thirteen major extinctions; civilization records many more. John Shea of Harvard University observes the pattern of life and emphasizes that everything must eventually face this reality. The modern human population's current genes and features will cease to exist. It is the fate of every species and of every technology.

Continual innovation is essential to life and competitive organizations, but it is not enough. We must be able to make the best use of our time and technology. People hate change—so use it sparingly. The Cambrian logic shows us a potential way of maximizing technological change and perhaps maximizing its impact. *Lumpy* or discontinuous change seems to be far superior to continual change.

# REFERENCES

Burke, James. 1978. *Connections.* Boston: Little, Brown & Co.: 204–20.

Coyne, William E. 1996. Building a tradition of innovation. *UK Innovation Lecture,* 5 May, 1, 5–8.

Hall, R. W. 1983. *Zero inventories.* Homewood, Ill.: Dow Jones-Irwin, 197.

High-tech companies get more for R&D dollar. 1995. *Industrial Engineering* (December): 11.

Kennedy, Paul. 1987. The (relative) decline of America. *Atlantic Monthly* (August): 29–38.

Langer, E. J., and L. Imber. 1979. When practice makes imperfect: The debilitating effects of overlearning. *Journal of Personality and Social Psychology* 37: 2014–25.

Lesson, Don. 1992. *Kings of creation.* Simon & Schuster, 104.

Mass, Nathaniel J., and Peter M. Senge. 1981. Reindustrialization: Aiming at the right targets. *Technology Review* (August/September): 56–65.

Newtson, D. 1973. Attribution and the unit of perception of ongoing behavior. *Journal of Personality and Social Psychology* 28: 1, 28–38.

Schonberger, R. J. 1982. *Japanese manufacturing practices.* New York: Free Press.

Successful organizations integrate primary functions. *Industrial Engineering* (December): 10.

Tuchman, Barbara W. 1979. *A distant mirror: The calamitous 14th century.* New York: Ballantine Books.

Tyre, Marcie J., and Wanda J. Orlikowski. 1993. Exploring Opportunities for technological improvement in organization. *Sloan Management Review* 35, no. 1 (fall): 13–17.

# CHAPTER 11

# Anticipating and Understanding Change:
# Phase Planes—A New Tool

## INTRODUCTION

Chaos theory and quantum mechanics tell us about the probabilistic nature of our world, where predictability is impossible. But all is not lost. Exact events are unpredictable, but a general pattern of "basins of attraction" does exist. This chapter describes this pattern and shows how to calculate it by using *phase planes*. It is this tool that improves your understanding of your business environment and sensitivity to changes in it. It also helps you to identify your liquid-like **zone of creativity.**

It is one thing to conceive of an innovation or find a creative solution to a problem; it is quite another to understand how to implement it. The next three chapters examine this process. It begins with developing a better understanding and sensitivity to how change itself is occurring. A good place to start comes from a field originally restricted to the mathematical field. This study is often called chaos theory or the sciences of complexity.

As already discussed, chaos theory and the field of complexity show us that complex actions can come from simple rules, and that complex interactions can create simple patterns of behavior. Business is the very definition of complexity because there are a great many independent agents interacting with each other in a great many ways. Chaos theory can help us to develop simple rules to deal with a complex world and can help us to discover simple patterns of interactions between us, our competition, customer, cost, and how to best anticipate and adapt to changes in them. It can do this because it can teach us about reality, not what we would like but rather what really exists out there.

The dark side of chaos theory tells us that initial order can unravel into unpredictability so you cannot predict very far. On the other hand, it also says that things

113

that look completely disordered may be predictable over the short term. Long term is unpredictable, but in the short term there exists order within disorder. This being the case, it is possible to find underlying patterns in chaotic systems that can be used to make good predictions. This is good news for managers because you do not have to look very far into the future to make a useful prediction. Even a little bit of information can be helpful. You can make a good guess about one move ahead.

Ralph Stacy, professor of management at the University of Hertfordshire Business School in the United Kingdom (UK), says that chaos theory offers a way of talking about what goes on inside organizations and making sense of a world in great uncertainty. He believes that the theory's most valuable insight is the complete unpredictability of the behavior of most systems, whether in nature or business.

## PREDICTABILITY IS IMPOSSIBLE, SO REMAIN FLEXIBLE

Most managers know that long-term plans rarely materialize, so if that is the case, why do we make them? Chaos theory, according to Barry Johnson, former head of Northern Telecom's training institute and now a consultant, says that companies should reexamine what they can and cannot control. Stacy says that such reevaluations have caused some companies to drop some longer-term planning processes altogether. Jim Cooper, human resource planner with Shell group's petroleum engineering division, says chaos theory asks useful questions about the reasonableness or otherwise of trying to predict the future (Applications of Chaos 1995).

The theory's value is that it can give us a deeper understanding of how our organization and our business environment works. To achieve this greater understanding we first must accept some facts of life. One of these is the fact about what is and is not controllable. As noted, chaos theory shows us that strict control and prediction in business is useless and, as such, undermines the business wisdom that we can control things by our sheer will and vision. Management that gets together at a retreat and constructs its vision for where it wants to be in 10 years is merely attending a social gathering—not a strategy session. It is better to focus on being reactive, not proactive. Stacy notes that elaborate computer-modeled forecasts presented to the board to convince them of the wisdom of a proposed business venture are a fiction and that their purpose should be to allay anxiety rather than perform any genuinely predictive purpose (Applications of Chaos 1995). The best we can hope for, it seems, is to remain as flexible as possible. Like the chess strategy mentioned earlier, analyze possible alternatives and choose options that give you the greatest adaptability because the long-term future is basically uncontrollable.

The need to innovate is constant, its consequences unforeseen and not subject to strict control or accurate prediction. Perhaps the only certainty is knowing that staying the same or going through too much change is courting disaster. A certain amount of instability is essential for creativity to exist. Simon Caulkin, editor of *The Observer* notes, "Attempts to make the system (organizations) stable work only at the expense of making it incapable of interacting with the environment . . .the result is stagnation and death" (Caulkin 1995). It is what we referred to earlier as reaching a state of equilibrium. Such systems or those closed to new input cannot continue to exist. Viable system thinking, organizations or otherwise, must have some instability. The message for managers is to accept uncontrollable change as a natural part of life. Change, for the most part, cannot be ordered, controlled, or predicted.

This book has constantly emphasized the need to be sensitive to your environment. It is the only way to determine the degree of creativity and innovation that needs to exist so that you can remain competitive. The value of chaos theory and its counterpart, complexity science, is that it can help business leaders to discover simple patterns of interactions between us, our competition, customer, cost, and how to best anticipate and adapt to changes in them. It is true that chaos theory says initial order can unravel into unpredictability so you cannot predict very far. Long term is unpredictable but in the short term there exists order within disorder. It is possible to find underlying patterns in a chaotic business environment that can be used to make good predictions. Even a little bit of information can be helpful, even in a chaotic world.

# EVOLUTION AND SELF-ORGANIZATION

Darwin said humans, like other animals, were the result of accidental mutations. Those creatures that survived were most fit for their environments. Humans, it seems, were the chance outcome of some common ancestors that existed in the Cambrian explosion 550 million years ago. One thought that is often used to describe evolution was fashioned by biologist Jacques Monod who said, "Evolution is chance caught on the wing" (Kauffman 1995, 17). Darwin would have us believe that we and all the other creatures around us are accidental. Start all over again and, in all likelihood, humans would never exist at all. We are, according to evolution, very lucky to be here.

The science of complexity and self-organization, however, has proposed that evolution's natural selection alone is not enough to explain all the order we see around us. Darwin, it seems, had it almost right! He was smart, but was unable to see the deeper order underlying evolution. Evolution only works on those things that natural existing order creates. The science of complexity and chaos theory says we are not accidental but rather the expected result, like in the sand pile, there is spontaneous or natural order in the universe. Darwin's natural selection and other evolutionary principles only come into play after life self-organizes and emerges. Evolution acts upon the raw materials that spontaneous order creates. It is natural selection and nature's own self-organizational predisposition that explain the order we see around us.

Even though evolutionary concepts have been around for awhile, the realization that spontaneous order underlies this biology is a relatively recent proposition. There are strong indications that it exists but it has not been proven, at least to the degree of Darwin's evolution. Clearly, nature does exhibit spontaneous order that can be seen from an ink droplet in water that naturally forms a sphere to the consistent shape of sand dunes in a desert. Each cell of your body must coordinate the activities of 100,000 genes and the enzymes and proteins they produce. Order, it seems, is everywhere around and in us. The cause of this natural occurring order is of intense interest to many physicists, biologists, and other theoretical scholars, but it's mechanics that holds practical benefits and risk for organizational leaders and managers.

# EVOLVING WORK SYSTEMS

Understanding how life, our organizations, and other complex adaptive systems work is essential for our survival and it begins, of all places, with the study of quantum mechanics and chaos theory. The discovery of quantum mechanics was a great discovery for mankind but, unfortunately, it is extremely difficult to understand. Both chaos theory and quantum mechanics try to help us understand the fundamental laws of the universe within which we live. Both are most applicable to the very large (behavior of universe) and very small (elementary particles). The lessons drawn from these descriptions will continue to emerge for centuries to come, but we already know some of the answers.

Albert Einstein could never accept the implications of quantum mechanics and once muttered that "God does not play die with the universe." Quantum mechanics shows us that Einstein was wrong. Quantum mechanics teaches us that life is not deterministic but rather is probabilistic. We can never be sure of outcomes; small changes in a quantum world can have enormous differences based on simple random chance. Life works this way and, as a result, we cannot predict the behavior of the universe nor much within it. Of course, this is no news to the everyday Joe, but such thinking has led to deeper rethinking about how things work and how best to function within the universe.

# SELF-ORGANIZING ORDER

As noted in chapter 2, the second law of thermodynamics states that entropy occurs in isolated, closed, or equilibrium systems. Closed systems produce continual disintegration of randomness, whereas open or creative systems overcome entropy by constantly interacting with its environment. Organizations and our minds, unlike closed systems, are open systems and make use of disorder to create chances for growth. Unlike computers, they are capable of maintaining an identity while changing form (Stumpf 1995). There is control, but it is of a fluid self-organizing nature that continues to evolve.

As new information enters an organization or our own minds, the information is incorporated if it supports it. If new information is perceived as threatening, our minds system tries to accommodate the information by making small changes that are consistent with the past. It tries to maintain its pattern of existence. Order is maintained, but the reaction to this new information is not predictable. The **pattern** tends to be maintained, but the exact shape cannot be predicted. Here there is general rather than rigid control.

There is useful information here. Our minds and our organizations are able to adapt to their environment but must accept the fact that exact control over such a system is impossible. Rigid control for creative entities removes its ability to respond to its environment. How do you control such a creature—the answer is, you don't. Feedback and communication from the environment provides the indirect control. Normally, control implies that you do not need to know this (information), creative systems emphasize *you need to know this* so you can respond to changes and new stimuli. Organizations and our minds are both unpredictable yet bounded at the same time. This means that each never reaches a true equilibrium because each is very sensitive to small disturbances at any time. On the other hand, these systems never go beyond certain limits or boundaries; it is the basins of attraction to which a system eternally returns. We all have our basins of attraction, we all seek the status quo—that is one reason why true change is so hard to accomplish.

Organizations, our minds, and other so-called nonlinear systems tend to gravitate toward these patterns of behavior. Such patterns are nonlinear because although each action is never exactly or precisely repeated, but a general pattern of behavior does emerge. A human heart is one such nonlinear system because no two beats are exactly the same. Although each beat tends to be similar to the one before, no two are exactly alike. As a result, a pattern of heartbeats emerges that helps the body maintain reasonable stability. Serious problems occur if a heartbeat or organization leaves its basin of attraction. The system can immediately become chaotic! It is as if the system is lost and is unable to find and reestablish its normal pattern. Whenever this occurs, performance can become highly unpredictable. Chaos theory can give business leaders new ways of analyzing their organization and its interaction with change in the business environment. To use them, though, requires a willingness to have flexible control that allows some variances.

# PHASE PLANES

Our minds as well as our organizations create simple patterns whenever each interacts with its environment. Patterns emerge as our complex organizations try to exist between the status quo and random chaos and change. The closer one is to the edge of chaos, the more irregular this interaction or pattern becomes.

One of these newer chaos-inspired or nonlinear tools is called phase plane *analysis*. It is a tool that describes the "evolving state" of these open systems. A phase plane is a visual tool that describes the change conditions of any system by identifying its "current location on a common two-dimensional Cartesian plane" (Priesmeyer and Cole 1995, 2). The two dimensions you want to measure are plotted on a graph and the outcome is that a pattern of interactions emerges. Phase planes can help business leaders to see patterns of interactions that are occurring within their business environment. Business ratios are a good source of such data. These ratios can be plotted on phase planes to show changes in production efficiency, quality control, or any common financial ratio. The picture or pattern that emerges can be seen and analyzed so that you see the dynamics or stability of your work environment. It can be used to generally predict what you can and cannot reasonably expect; and it can be used to solve a number of problems that were heretofore hard to visualize.

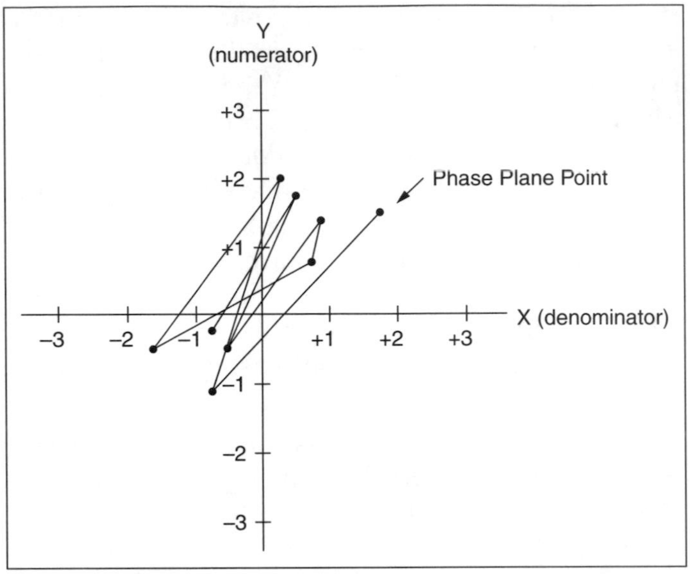

**Figure 11.1.**
Basic "Phase Plane"

Phase planes like those in Figures 11.1 and 11.3 plot changes in two measures. They plot the differences between each measure value and its value in the previous period. Changes can be either positive or negative from one period to another. The center of the phase plane is coordinate 0,0. It represents no change in either measure, quadrants are traditionally numbered counterclockwise starting in the upper right quadrant. The evolving "state of a system" is plotted on phase planes. Each measure being plotted will change over time and those changes are plotted incrementally.

Phase planes show the interaction of two variables over the same time period. Each axis is used to plot the changes in one of these measures. Points on the phase plane represent changes in the relationship between these two measures ($X$ and $Y$). Connecting these points allows you to identify the trajectory or pattern of interaction occurring within a system.

Financial ratios have traditionally been used with phase planes because they give you two variables ($X$ and $Y$) showing a system's activity. One becomes the numerator ($Y$) and the other becomes the denominator ($X$). Actually, ratio or any other data is not plotted but rather the **changes** in the data over time is plotted. Differences between these consecutive numbers can be either positive or negative.

Production, inventory, or quality variables can be plotted on the phase plane. Several such ratios are noted in the Innovative IQ Questionnaire (see Exercise 5 in chapter 14). Potential ratios that could be plotted are noted by asterisks. Phase planes are initially divided into four equal quadrants. Each of these quadrants, as seen in Figure 11.2, represents specific behaviors of any two interactive measures (for example, income to sales).

| Change in Y | |
|---|---|
| Quadrant 2 | Quadrant 1 |
| (decrease in X, increase in Y) | (increase in both measures) |
| | Change in X |
| Quadrant 3 | Quadrant 4 |
| (decrease in both measures) | (increase in X, decrease in Y) |

**Figure 11.2.**
Quadrants of a Phase Plane

Generally, over time, you will begin to see data accumulate in more than one quadrant. Points appearing in both quadrants 1 and 3 are moving in the same direction because both $X$ and $Y$ are either increasing (quadrant 1) or decreasing (quadrant 3). Data appearing primarily in quadrants 2 and 4 are primarily moving in opposite directions.

Figure 11.3 shows a phase plane with most of the activity occurring in quadrants 1 and 3. This type of phase plane is called a two-period phase plane because the oscillation is primarily between these two or any two areas of the graph.

The points of a phase plane, as seen in Figure 11.3, represent changes in two measures of change in one type of defect (numerator) to change in total defects (denominator). The lines connecting these points are tracking these points as they move through time. Connecting points on a phase plane creates its trajectory. Several lines, as in Figure 11.3, create a system's evolving pattern or its "basin of attraction." When phase planes are plotted, you begin to see patterns emerge. It is the patterns that show you the specific changes that are occurring. Because each quadrant identifies unique changes (in this case, it's changes in one type of defect to total defects), it means that you can interpret the results and make both predictive and prescriptive decisions. For instance, we can choose to plot the changes in one type of defect, say the diameter of a hole ($Y$ variable) to the changes in the total number of defects occurring in a process.

Points appearing in quadrant 1 indicate that both this particular defect and total defects were increasing. Figure 11.3 provides a perfect two-period phase plane, except for the last point where your changes in total defects decreased but your changes in diameter of a hole increased. A business ratio of .5 will create an angle of 45° (see dashed line). A 45° angle or isoquant shows a stable pattern where both $X$ and $Y$ are increasing or decreasing proportionally. This .5 ratio is the

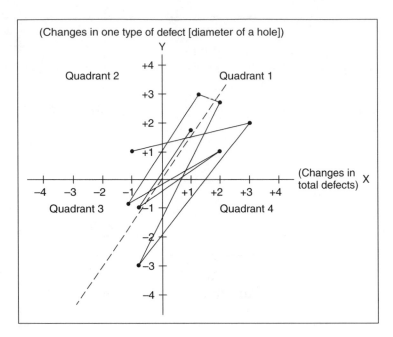

**Figure 11.3.**
A Two-period Phase Plane

difference between each of the two variables that are being compared. It essentially indicates very good stability; total defects occurring and defects in diameter of a hole (in this case) go up and down together. When variables go up and down together, you have a stable pattern. Generally, that is what is happening in Figure 11.3. A ratio of 1/3 produces an isoquant of 30° and still indicates a stable pattern. Another way of saying this is that generally the defects in hole diameter increase or decrease as total defects increase or decrease, but not as closely as when the pattern was a 45° isoquant.

Phase planes provide better information for business leaders than simple business, manufacturing, or service ratios because they reveal more information about the business. They can be used to understand the changes in the relationship between Y and X (one defect to another, income to sales, and so on), which cannot be seen by simply looking at ratios. Phase planes are dynamic; ratios are static. They are better because a great deal of information is lost in ratio. For instance, each of your two measures can increase, decrease, or remain the same. That is nine possible states (for example, $3 \times 3 = 9$). A ratio can only increase, decrease, or remain the same. That is only three states or a 66 percent reduction in information. This means the decision-maker would be making choices, implementing actions, and diverting resources for less knowledge (66 percent to be exact) than if he or she had used phase planes rather than ratios.

## CALCULATING PHASE PLANES

Points on any phase plane are calculated by comparing the differences or changes in a value from one period to the next. A simple example of some phase plane calculations is seen in Figure 11.4.

| | (X) Total Number of Defects | Marginal Difference | (Y) Diameter Defects | Marginal Difference |
|---|---|---|---|---|
| Period 1 | 20 | | 8 | |
| | | > ────────► +5 | | +4 |
| Period 2 | 25 | | 12 | |

**Figure 11.4.**
Calculations for Phase Plane

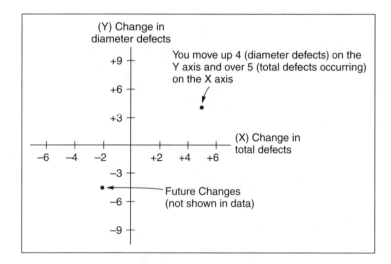

**Figure 11.5**
Graphing Points on a Phase Plane

Each of these marginal difference numbers becomes a point that is plotted, on a phase plane, like that in Figure 11.5. Each phase plane is scaled to allow for the largest marginal value in a set of numbers. Each of these numbers (for example, +5 and +4 in Figure 11.4) is then indexed on the graph (see point in quadrant 1) in Figure 11.5. A trajectory is produced when you draw a line from each succeeding point (see point in quadrant 3). Several lines and points produce a picture that shows how your relationship (in this case, between diameter defects and overall defects occurring in process) is changing over time.

## READING PHASE PLANES

Information plotted over time on a phase plane will produce one of several patterns. Figure 11.6 shows a highly unusual pattern where there is no change. The data, called period 1 stability, is completely stable (no change over time in $X$ and $Y$). Obviously such an event in the real world would be extremely rare but would represent the very visual definition of the status quo.

Two-point trajectories, like that already seen in Figure 11.3, are the more common way that ratios or other related production data oscillate. For instance, production to income or sales, volume of inventory to sales, cycle time to sales, and so

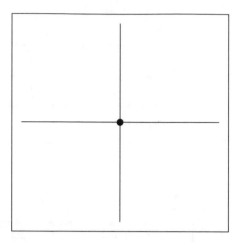

**Figure 11.6.**
Period 1 Stability

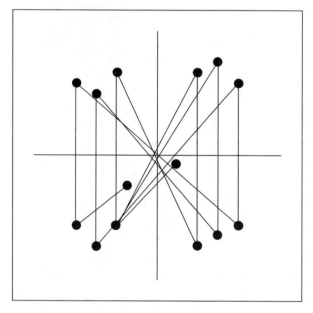

**Figure 11.7.**
4 Period Oscillation

forth would often yield a two-point trajectory. In other words, they both go up (diameter defects up, total defects in process up) and down together. Therefore, the things causing one problem are those affecting the other. More complex oscillations are also possible when you have a great number of assignable causes that are unique to one variable (Y) and not to the other (X). Figure 11.7 shows a 4 period oscillation. This type of pattern occurs whenever one measure is oscillating or changing twice as fast as the other. It tends to create a slightly out of sync "figure

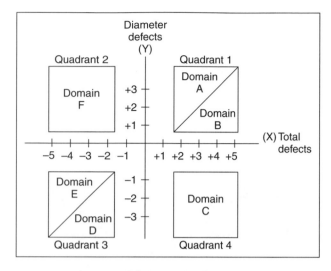

**Figure 11.8.**
Domains of Phase Planes

8's" appearance. Actual trajectories for real companies are often less clear-cut but a general pattern does tend to emerge. Random fluctuations that are all over the grid is an example of chaos.

It is possible to understand the general changes that are occurring in a phase plane, by examining the domain of a quadrant. Figure 11.8 provides an example of how to read one of these phase planes where *Y* represents diameter defects and *X* is total defects.

Beginning on the right side and proceeding clockwise you first see domain A in quadrant 1. Data that appear in this area indicate that the number of diameter defects is increasing faster than your total defects. Data appearing in B indicate that total defects rather than diameter defects is increasing faster. This C domain would mean total defects would be increasing but diameter defects is decreasing. Even though both diameter defects and total defects are decreasing in D, diameter defects are declining more rapidly. In E both diameter defects and total defects are declining but total defects, rather than diameter defects, are decreasing more rapidly. The last domain of F shows total defects declining and diameter defects increasing. In other words, you are getting better overall but diameter defects are becoming an increasing problem.

## UNDERSTANDING CHANGE

This book has emphasized the need to become sensitive to changes in one's environment. We have also stated the importance of remaining within the zone of creativity, which is between the edge of chaos and rigid stability. Phase planes show the degree of change (chaos) or stability occurring within its business environment. They also can be used to better understand those changes occurring within

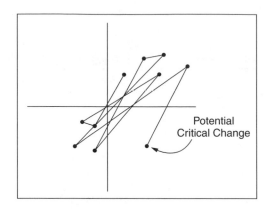

**Figure 11.9.**
Visual Proof of a Critical Change

an organization, or as an early warning of critical changes that are developing. It is these relative changes that are occurring that are most important. The unit of analysis is completely arbitrary and up to the manager's discretion to decide what relationship between what two variables are most relevant to their business. Quality or production ratios or changes usually indicate relevant data to plot on phase planes but any data and its relevant changes can be plotted on them. Figure 11.9 shows a normal stable pattern as well as a critical change that could be potentially developing (see quadrant 4). It is just such a change that can cause a stable system to become chaotic. It can be a forewarning of serious or catastrophic changes that are beginning to occur in your production process.

The reality is that every point on a phase plane represents a specific change between two variables (one defect to another, inventory to sales, and so on). As with ratios, no single measure or point can provide you with enough information. The important point to remember is that you can infer something is happening only when you see those measures changing over time. It is the degree of that change and how those changes are occurring that is most important.

Phase planes not only focus on what is happening now, they also help you understand why the change is happening to your business or department and, just as importantly, what you can do about it. You could compare your sales to your inventory levels or inventory turnover or even compare your cycle time versus inventory or you could compare productivity numbers to those of your major competitors. Phase planes thus allow you to look internally or externally and evaluate a wide range of inventory, production, waste, or quality issues.

Once you have collected information on why the productivity, inventory, cost, or quality change is occurring, you can then prescribe some action. Phase planes provide you with better information and that makes prescribing what to do both easier and clearer. They help you to see recent changes and in turn make it easier to determine future directions.

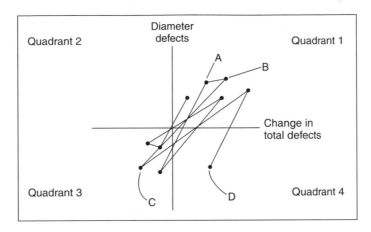

**Figure 11.10.**
Phase Plane for Diameter Defects

# PHASE PLANES REVIEW

Phase planes can be used to provide useful reports to the shop floor. For instance, quality control can use them to identify special and common causes of variation. Special causes in quality control refer to unusual variation or changes that are not expected. Common variation would include the normal oscillations in quality even though it is still "in control." Here is how it might work.

The phase plane provides specific interpretations for each quadrant. Quadrants 1 and 3 data indicate near proportional changes between any defect (like the diameter defect mentioned earlier) and total defects. Quadrant 2 (upper left) is very important because it shows a particular defect is increasing while total defects is declining. This is telling you that this defect is a *major* barrier to improvements. It requires intervention in order to improve the process. If the data is mainly confined to quadrant 4, then you know that the defect is declining while other defects are increasing. Intervention here would be good so you can identify why it is declining. You may be looking at an opportunity to discover and implement the same situation within other areas. Phase planes can show a typical pattern as in Figure 11.10, but they can also show, again as seen in Figure 11.9, unexpected or potential critical change points. When this occurs, it is time to identify the reason for the decrease.

On point A in quadrant 1, the ratio of diameter defects to total defects increases. One way to interpret this is to say even though both diameter defects and total defects are rising, the change in diameter defects is rising faster. The next point B seems to reinforce this conclusion. One recommendation could be to immediately examine the *cause* of increased diameter defects. Likewise, when the process visits quadrant 3, as was the case for C, you can interpret this to say that a decrease in diameter defects contributed some to the reduction in total defects. A recommendation might be to look for the underlying cause of both diameter

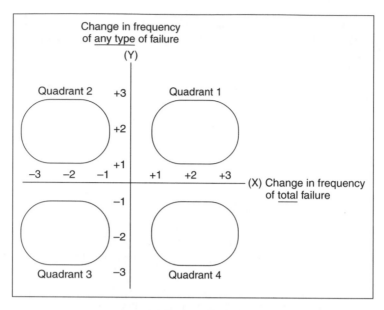

**Figure 11.11.**
Phase Planes as a Quality Tool

defects and total defects. When quadrant 4 is visited, as seen by D, you can assume in this case that an individual defect and total defects do not appear to be directly related. Here total defects are increasing but diameter defects are decreasing. One recommendation would be to look at other sources to explain the increase in total defects.

Let's assume another situation. A phase plane can be constructed like that seen in Figure 11.11. It is comparing the changes in total failures for a process on the $X$ axis to the change in frequency of a particular type of failure on the $Y$ axis. For sake of discussion, let's assume we are comparing the total number of failures for a process to those failures that are due to machine breakdowns.

If you find that your points are occurring mainly in quadrant 1, then both are increasing. Now suppose that you introduce a preventative maintenance program (PM) to help solve these process failures. Assume the next data you receive then appears in quadrent 4. Data appearing in quadrant 4 shows that machine breakdowns are decreasing while total failures are still increasing. If this is truly the situation, then you know that it is helping reduce machine breakdowns, but not significantly affecting or reducing your overall process failures. Something else is causing those problems.

On the other hand, if you discover that most of the data is now appearing in quadrant 2, then you can assume that your PM program is having little or minimum effect on machine breakdowns. In other words, overall process failures are down but machine breakdowns are up. You know at least two things. First, your PM program is not working, and, second, future machine breakdowns are likely to remain a major barrier to further improvement in process reliability. If you find that the data oscillate between quadrant 1 and quadrant 3, then you can assume one type of failure (machine breakdowns) is directly related to overall process failures. It is a *common cause* of variation because one type of failure increases or decreases in direct proportion to increases or decreases in total failures.

Finally, if the data show a phase plane where all four quadrants are regularly being visited, then you know there is little, if any, association between increases or decreases in machine breakdowns and corresponding increases or decreases in overall process failures. Such a loose connection between these two variables means you will have to search for more unique or *assignable causes.*

Your job just got a lot harder because you can assume that several things may be causing these wild fluctuations in reliability. Other avenues might include changing the process itself, using new materials, training personnel, or experimenting with new equipment. Each new change and its effect can be seen on the phase plane, and the results can be read depending on what quadrants are visited.

Phase planes can show relationships between an overall variable and one particular variable like the impact of a PM program. They can also be used to discover if there are relationships between two particular types of variables. Assume you want to see if there is a relationship between defects in alignment of a part and say the material defects. Plot one on the *X* axis and the other on the *Y* axis. If your data tends to primarily visit quadrants 1 and 3, rather than all quadrants, then a relationship does exist. Because these two quality problems have a common connection, you can affect one by affecting the other so there is a common cause relationship. On the other hand, the more points visit all quadrants, the less relationship exists between the two. There are special or assignable causes affecting the different variables.

# SUMMARY

A key concept for improving creativity is to create nonequilibrium systems that operate in the creative zone between chaos and order. As mentioned earlier, you can have too much chaos, but you can also have too much order. The trick is to stay in the middle between the edge of static equilibrium and the edge of chaos.

Organizations, departments, and creative minds must maintain a certain amount of internal order, but it is order that requires a constant source of energy similar to a whirlpool bath. The swirl of water can be stable for a long time provided water is continually added to the tub and the drain is left open. The flow or movement of this matter and energy is the essential driving force behind order in the universe. When the flow stops, the system reaches equilibrium and ceases to exist.

We should try for a liquid state between order and chaos similar to the stages of water. Water exists in three phases—ice, liquid, and steam. We need to be in the middle or between the edge of chaos and the edge of equilibrium. *Ice* organizations are frozen by being too far into the ordered regime; *gas* organizations are in a chaotic state constantly being ripped apart by change. Many organizations and perhaps even minds are deeply frozen in the ordered state and will soon perish because they cannot adapt to changes in their environment.

Phase planes help a business know the general pattern of changes that are emerging and can help you understand your degree of stability or instability and perhaps give you these precious few moments where you can rapidly react to sudden changes. They provide practical, down-to-earth, real-time information, something that the normal, cold, static business ratios are unable to achieve.

Tools like chaos theory and phase planes help us to better understand change and your business's general pattern of behavior in the face of these changes. They help you to compare how you are doing in relation to your major competitors. They can help you to better understand and manage your business process by providing more real-time information about quality, productivity, competitive, or consumer problems.

# REFERENCES

Applications of chaos. 1995. *Management Today* (July): 17.

Caulkin, Simon. 1995. Chaos Inc. *Across the Board* (July/August): 34.

Kauffman, Stuart. 1995. *At home in the universe: The search for laws of self-organization and complexity.* New York: Oxford University Press.

Order from chaos. 1994. *Management Today* (November): 65.

Priesmeyer, H. Richard, and Edward G. Cole. 1995. Phase plane analysis: A nonlinear way to track quality. 3rd Annual *Chaos in Manufacturing* Conference. Santa Fe, New Mexico, April 11–15, 1–10.

Stumpf, Stephen A. 1995. Applying new science theories in leadership development activities. *Journal of Management Development* 14, no. 5 (May): 39–49.

# CHAPTER 12

# Directing Relevant Innovation Efforts

## INTRODUCTION

The risk of ignoring irrelevant innovation has already been discussed. Given enough time and money most everything is possible. Limitation often forces us to prioritize and focus on a few critical innovations to pursue. Innovations of most value are those that most clearly relate to the company's vision. Such a vision, to be a useful guide for innovation, must be more than a paper statement. It should relate to employees' human component. It must inspire them. Only then can you understand and assess the trade-offs needed to make it work.

Frances Hesselbein runs the Drucker Foundation. Hesselbein was CEO of the Girl Scouts and was able to turn that troubled organization around by increasing membership and dramatically increasing participation by minorities. As a result, she created a vibrant and creative organization. So how did she do it? She said, "We changed everything about the Girl Scouts, challenging every policy, practice and procedure, but never its values, never its mission" (who they were) (Sherman 1995, 90–96).

> ## IMPRINT YOUR VALUES ON YOUR GROUP

3M has basic requirements they feel are essential for building a tradition of innovation. J. Marc Adams, vice president of marketing at 3M, notes that one of their central challenges is to understand how to innovate in the right way. Adams points out that 3M believes it is imperative to declare the importance of innovation and make it a part of a company's self-image. He asks, "How do we innovate and change in a way that is fast, constant and consistent with our values?" (Adams 1997). He believes it can only occur when your response is automatic or instinctive. They believe it is management's responsibility to continually remind all employees that all efforts should be directed toward validating this vision. In an organization, knowing who you are comes from operating from a tradition. This tradition is a set of behaviors that is so ingrained that people don't really have to think about it. Adams feels this is 3M's great unquantifiable strength.

# CLARIFY WHY IT'S IMPORTANT

Leaders trying to encourage innovation first need to survey the organization. Many will discover that their organization is probably a pretty good, but not great one. The usual reaction involves trying to create both a vision and feedback by identifying where you want to go, which might be to try to deliver great customer service. What is often missing is a commitment to make sure that personnel are not a roadblock (don't crash into each other) or are flying off in all sorts of directions. Where many fail is that we often do not do a good job of explaining to each person where they specifically fit in and how they are doing. If you want people to care, to think, and to find new solutions, then they must be sold on why it is important. One way to do this is by (1) describing the realities about where we are headed, (2) identifying a common direction or focus about what we are supposed to be doing, and (3) identifying why it is relevant to employees.

Vision is more than simply printing so many words on a piece of paper. If you want to tap that wellspring of creative energy, then you have to say something that compels or inspires people. It has to make them feel bigger than they are and that, generally, has to be more than simply making money for someone else. For instance, Southwest Airlines' personnel do not believe they are working for simply a low-cost airline. Rather many truly believe they are in the business of freedom. Management has convinced many that they are on a crusade to open up the skies and give ordinary people the chance to see and do things they never dreamed of. They are innovating and finding creative solutions so those who could not fly can now fly. Ron Ricks, Southwest's vice president of governmental affairs, says they see their job as a higher calling. They ask themselves, "How can we protect small businesses? Are we doing what's best for the senior citizens who count on us for low fares?" John Denison, Southwest's vice president of corporate services, says, "The product we deliver is a wonderful contribution to society. We make it possible for people to fly who could never afford to fly in the past" (Freiberg and Freiberg 1996, 10–11).

---

### INSPIRE INDIVIDUALS

---

Stock analysts love Medtronic, a medical products company located in Minneapolis, because employees turn out so many new innovations. A full 50 percent of revenues come from products introduced in the past 12 months. The company's total return to shareholders has averaged about 34 percent annually over the past decade. Bill George, CEO of Medtronic, says, "Shareholder value is a hollow notion as the sole source of employee motivation. If you do business that way, you end up like ITT" (Lieber 1998).

Medtronic is a profitable company, but what really gets their people fired up is not about making money but is rather about who they are, which they believe is *helping sick people get well.* Employees at the company keep their focus on people who have the company's products implanted inside them. Companies like Merck and Medtronic have long understood the importance of defining who we are in relation to what their people think is important. Medtronic's motto is, "Restoring patients to full life." Its symbol is a supine human rising toward upright wellness. This imagery comes to life each December at the company's holiday party when patients are flown in to tell their survival stories. Journalists are generally not invited. Employees, year after year, are moved to tears. Art Collins, 50, a strong guy with a firm handshake, is not prone to crying fits. He said, "I assumed I'd be fine, but then these parents got up with their daughter who was alive because of our products. Even surgeons who see this stuff all the time were crying" (Lieber 1998).

Inspiration can also come in other ways. John Mackey, who helped start Whole Foods Market, a chain of natural foods groceries, says that their clearly stated mission has helped him draw motivated employees who are more educated than the typical grocery worker. Lisa Shaw, 30, is an example. She is a Wellesley College graduate who works in Brighton, Massachusetts, for one of the company's Bread and Circus Stores. She says she sees the looks on people's faces when she tells them what she is doing. She says, "I just hang on to the fact that my job is good in some larger sense, which I believe is helping people live healthier lives. If people buy the sprouts, they're eating healthier foods, the farmer is doing well, and it's good for the plant because they're grown organically" (Lieber 1998). Such high-minded talk and motivation can only occur if the company clearly defines who they are and, just as importantly, if that definition taps into their people's humanity. People at Johnson and Johnson, Medtronic, and Whole Foods make the explicit connections between their company's financial success and its larger goal of making a difference. It is this connection that ultimately leads others to want to find new solutions and innovate.

## MEASURING INNOVATION

If you want innovation, you must measure it, but be sure you are measuring the right things. Measuring the wrong performance is even worse than not having any measures at all. The story of the Dead Sea Scrolls is an excellent example of inappropriate rewards producing inappropriate behavior. When the first Dead Sea Scrolls were discovered and archaeologists wanted more scraps of the scrolls to be found and turned in by wandering Arab shepherds, the misguided scholars offered a fixed reward *per scrap,* thereby making it likely that the fragments would be broken up into tiny pieces before it was delivered. Incentives provide selection pressures and determine which behavior is appropriate.

Measuring the degree of cost efficiencies, profits, or productivity will encourage innovative thinking in these areas. Measurement should relate to what you want your people to think about. If it is important to find new ways of offering great customer service, then measure it. All too often we use measures of performance, but just as often these very measures distract rather than enhance innovativeness.

## INNOVATION MUST RELATE TO KEY SUCCESS VARIABLES

The Swedish ABB Corporation provides a good example of how to design good feedback on performance. To be competitive, management at ABB felt that it was necessary to increase speed by reducing cycle times by 50 percent. They created their innovative T-50 program that reduced order and other cycle times by an average of 40 percent. One of their keys to these improvements was changing from activity-related objectives, like the count of company seminars or projects that have been authorized, to more results-oriented feedback, such as on-time delivery and reducing the cycle time for R and D. The new feedback system got people to begin thinking about finding new ways to increase speed. They realized a good way to do this was to measure cycle time. They reasoned that their new focus was speed, so it seemed logical to measure overall results (cycle time) rather than counting individual measures.

## FOCUS ON RESULTS-ORIENTED OBJECTIVES

General Electric (GE) provides another good illustration of both what to do as well as what not to do. GE is well known for using an innovative technique called *best practices*. This technique is similar to benchmarking because you identify the best practices of well-run companies. The difference is that best practices requires you to identify those best practices even if they are not in your field. Benchmarking tends to look at the nuts and bolts (For example, what can our shipping department learn from the shipping department at L.L. Bean?), but best practices is more concerned with broader management practices, issues, and attitudes.

GE's former director, James Baughman, said the key question they wanted answered was, "What is the secret of your success?" When GE looked at several companies, they discovered their best practices were remarkably similar. As with ABB, almost every company emphasized characteristics like managing the process, not the function. These companies also concentrated less on measuring the performance of individual departments and more on *results-oriented objectives* that focus people's thoughts in one direction. People began to look at and think about how the departments work together as products move from one area to another. It was during the process that GE realized they were setting goals and tracking performance but discovered that they were measuring the wrong things! George Zippil, the business development manager, said it best, "We should have focused more on what gets done (toward the vision) rather than how things get done (procedures)" (Steward 1991, 40–43).

A good example of this change in their measurement process and its effects can be seen in GE's reengineering efforts at their Evendale, Ohio, plant. A team at the plant constructed a process map that tracked the making of their turbine shafts for jet engines. The job took a month to do, but for the first time, GE had a coherent understanding of what was involved in the process from start to finish. John Chesson, the general manager of component manufacturing at Evendale, said it also changed opinions about what they should be measuring. Before they saw all the pieces put together, GE concentrated on measuring and managing worker and machine efficiency. Now they concentrate on what gets done in managing the results or what they call the *total asset*.

At one time, their goal was 100 percent machine utilization, so management required all of their rotating parts to be sent to a central steam-cleaning facility. By analyzing the operation, they discovered this process was both time-consuming and inefficient. They changed the way work was done, so rather than sending them to a central facility, machine operators now have their own cleaning booths. The result: the time saved more than paid for the additional equipment needed at each operation.

Effective innovation requires measuring things that directly relate to where you are going. GE began to recognize that machine utilization was only one piece of the picture. Previously, it had been a key measurement used to judge performance, so everyone focused on it. GE management soon realized a better approach would be to measure *results of something that gets done relative to the entire operation*. They did not want to focus on how things are done (for example, machine utilization) but rather on results or what gets done. One of their new goals, like ABBs, is to measure results by trying to reduce cycle time by 90 percent. Cycle time was defined as the total time from the moment a customer places an order until it is received. Reduction was to occur while still increasing the availability of customers getting what they wanted, which is another result or entire operation perspective.

## UNDERSTANDING TRADE-OFFS

Finding results-oriented goals that relate to the entire operation is one thing. But making sure that each goal builds on the other and does not send conflicting messages is another. No one is exactly sure how many is too many. In the previous example, GE used three goals (inventory turns, operating margins, and product development). At the operational level, most experts say that determining five specific goals is probably the maximum. Too many goals can distract from each other, so experts recommend prioritizing and consolidating.

Different goals or visions can pull people in different directions. Marketing ends up doing their own creative things and so too do production, finance, human resources, and so on. Progress is difficult if the production group is trying to figure out innovative solutions to increase yield or volume, while the engineering or marketing departments are concerned about something else. For innovation to be effective, goals and strategies must be well conceived and trade-offs of each goal analyzed. The purpose is to channel everyone's thoughts and efforts toward some unified direction.

## KNOW YOUR PRIORITIES AND TRADE-OFFS

Understanding our critical priorities is essential to the whole process. This will help insure that short-term decisions and activities are more consistent with long-term goals, like speed, customer service, or profits. Knowing our focus means knowing which innovative solutions should be pursued and which will be a secondary nature. Good *trade-off* analyses will involve determining what will be most difficult about reaching the goal, what goals will be in conflict, and how those conflicting goals should be ranked (Kauffman 1992, 84–85).

Understanding trade-offs is essential to good creativity. You can have innovation without assessing trade-offs, but often what you get is innovation of a haphazard nature that ultimately leads to disaster. When Lee Iacocca was president at Ford, they faced strong competition from Volkswagen. So top executives at Ford pushed the Pinto into production after only 2 years of development instead of the normal time span of about 43 months. Their own preproduction crash test had shown that rear-end collisions would rupture the Pinto's fuel system. Ford even owned the patent on a much safer fuel system, but senior officials decided to manufacture the car without making the safety changes. As a result, crashes involving Pintos have caused between 500 and 900 deaths to people who would not have been seriously injured if the car had not burst into flames (Silver and Mitchell 1990, 34–41).

Lee Iacocca set an operational goal known as the "limits of 2000," which meant that the Pinto was not to weigh an ounce over 2,000 pounds nor cost a cent over $2,000. All innovative plans for the car, including improved safety features for the gas tank, would have added both cost and weight to the car so they were rejected before they could be seriously evaluated.

Whenever innovation is being considered, you must address the trade-off necessary to accomplish the change. In order to attain greater speed, are you willing to have 2 or 3 months of operation below the old pace? When change is implemented, there is always a period of adjustment of a few months to years. Are you willing to accept that inefficiency? It takes time for people to be trained in how to improve speed, quality, or customer satisfaction. The more radical the innovation, the more dramatic the initial drop in performance. Before setting new goals, management must ask itself, "Are we willing to suffer these costs in order to reach our goal?" One innovation often leads to other changes. Departments and people will have to be eliminated, the way work is done will have to change, and what is done and not done will need to be reassessed.

Open discussion about both the impact of goals, expectations they create, and trade-offs that will be necessary is of utmost importance. In the end, such discussions will help everyone to better understand the trade-offs and avoid Pinto problems. Because the trade-offs may not be fully understood, weekly, or even daily, monitoring of quantifiable goals may be needed.

# SUMMARY

Knowing who you are and where you are going is essential if you hope to create useful and innovative thinking. Successful innovation demands a common direction. Good innovation demands, as J. Mark Adams of 3M says, that we innovate in a way that is consistent with our values. We must explain and sell our people on why it is important to find new solutions to old problems. Every effort must be made to inspire them to think in different ways.

But inspiration alone is not enough. Insuring that the right kinds of innovative thinking is occurring requires a relevant measurement system. The Swedish ABB Corporation found this system by focusing efforts around more results-oriented feedback like reducing cycle time for R and D. GE provides another example of what to do. They try to look at what gets done toward their vision rather than how it is done. They know innovation is only going to be effective if they judge ideas based on how each relates to where they are going. In their case, they want to know if the innovation helps them reduce cycle time or other entire operation perspectives.

The important point is to have a clear vision and know the trade-offs involved in achieving it. Prioritize actions and encourage, measure, and reward innovations in these directions. Finally, continually try to give people frequent feedback so they know what is happening, how they are doing, and what are their goals.

# REFERENCES

Adams, J. Marc. 1997. Competing in highly dynamic markets by strategic innovation: The 3M model. *1997 McGill Graduate Business Conference* (13 February): 6–7.

Freiberg, Kevin, and Jackie Freiberg. 1996. *Nuts! Southwest Airlines' crazy recipe for business and personal success.* Austin, Tex.: Bard Press, Inc., 4.

Kauffman, R. S. 1992. Why operations improvement programs fail, four managerial contradictions. *Sloan Management Review* (fall): 84–85.

Lieber, Ronald B. 1998. Why employees love these companies. *Fortune* 137, no. 1 (12 January): 74.

Sherman, Stratford. 1995. How tomorrow's best leaders are learning their stuff. *Fortune* 132, no. 11 (27 December): 90–96.

Silver, William S., and Terence R. Mitchell. 1990. The status quo tendency in decision making. *Organizational Dynamics* 18, no. 4 (spring): 34–41.

Steward, T. A. 1991. GE keeps those ideas coming. *Fortune* 124, no. 4 (12 April): 40–43.

# CHAPTER 13

# Leading Innovation

## INTRODUCTION

Implementing innovations requires forethought and much discussion. Seven rules are essential.

1. Ask what you are trying to do.
2. Get trust and buy-in from upper management.
3. Create disciples.
4. Measure and monitor the change.
5. Create dissatisfaction with the status quo.
6. Visualize a future state.
7. Tell people what is in it for them.

Glen H. Hiner, chairman and CEO of Owens-Corning, discussed the need to change in the face of ever-increasing global competition. At the same time he noted that it is human nature to fear change. We become comfortable with old habits, and we fear what we do not understand. Fear can be a powerful barrier.

Hiner said too many leaders assume that if they talk about the need to change enough, it somehow will automatically bring about improvements. Nothing could be farther from the truth. The bigger the organization, the more difficult it is to innovate. He pointed out that companies like Owens-Corning are a lot like battleships, rather than pleasure crafts. When you touch the control of a small entrepreneurial organization, it responds immediately, but it is another matter for battleships, like Owens-Corning. When you signal a change of course with these battleships, it takes a while before you notice any difference.

For this reason, Hiner believes timing is most important. If you wait until it is obvious to everyone that the company needs to change—you have waited too long. He insists that it is the leaders' responsibility to challenge themselves and others to innovate *before* there is a consensus that change is needed. You cannot dictate or demand improved productivity or better customer satisfaction. Your people must want to improve productivity or better customer satisfaction (Hiner 1994, 4).

# IMPLEMENTING INNOVATIONS

Implementing innovations can be an exhausting and frustrating experience. Nobody wants to change; we prefer the status quo even if it is bad. The difference between whether it is a very negative or positive experience is how the change is managed. When you ask managers who have been intimately involved in a project to describe their negative and positive experiences with change, it is almost always the same story. It is not so much what innovation is being implemented, but how it is done. Often, the first thing managers mention when asked to describe their negative experiences is the fact that those who try to implement the change do not take a unified approach. They often say that there was little foresight or planning. There was also unanimous agreement about the general lack of involvement and communication with those who will be affected by the change. As a result, there is little chance of buy-in. They are just informed of what they will be doing. Comments frequently heard make reference to creating a lose-lose situation. Exercise #6, in chapter 14, can help your people identify their own negative and positive experiences with change. The outcome of the exercise is to develop an action plan for your group so the next innovation is a positive experience.

If you do use this exercise, you will probably hear a group or individual describe a change that was dropped on them. People will say they felt powerless. Negative experiences with change often share one common attribute. Either they had no input or their recommendations were ignored. Frequently, there was not even an explanation about why the change was needed. There is minimum discussion of the problem and potential solutions. The outcome is predictable—a lack of trust. Gradually an atmosphere of dishonesty and personal paranoia develops that ultimately dooms the change.

When change works, it is an opposite or almost a mirror image of what happens when it does not work. There is a consistent, regular reporting of the status on the change so rumors can be kept to a minimum. Senior management, as chapter 12 recommends, has a clear vision for where they want to go. That is different from simply recognizing that some change is needed or that a problem exists. The innovators, often a project team, prioritize the details and decide what should be done and in what order. Effective change never requires that everybody become involved because that is clearly impossible. Rather successful change leaders define specific actions and commitments they need from key individuals. They work on obtaining this commitment and then communicating about the proposed change. This entails open explanation about why certain decisions are being made. It is not essential to get everyone involved but it is critical to show people what needs to be changed.

## RULE #1: ASK "WHAT ARE YOU TRYING TO DO?"

Assuming there is a need for an innovative solution, you will need a goal that is achievable. Having a realistic goal requires first identifying the area or issue that needs changing. Anyone who is seriously considering implementing a new change or innovation should consider reviewing Exercise #7 in chapter 14. It will give you a good guideline so that critical steps have been thought out. Exercise #8 is a more dynamic and fun exercise called "Play Cards for Change." This is a good exercise to use with a group of people to help them both reason out the process of change and discuss the right *sequence* that should be taken in implementing the change.

## RULE #2: CREATING TRUST AND BUY-IN—BEGIN AT THE TOP

The bigger the change, the more the CEO buy-in must be dramatic, consistent, and persistent. Someone once said that he could not believe the number of executives who quit smoking cigars when cigar-smoking Lee Iacocca retired as head of Chrysler. Employees naturally try to imitate their boss. The boss must buy-in. A good example of the power of initial commitment is demonstrated by Jerre Stead. He is currently the CEO for AT&T and is involved in trying to create a customer-focused organization. They have gone through a process of defining their mission, values, objectives, and strategies. The primary champion of this change is their CEO, Jerre Stead. When he speaks of creating a customer-focused organization, he knows that actions speak louder than words. To this end he spends an average of 2 days or 16 hours each week visiting customers. He also talks to approximately 15 customers by phone each week. When he talks to them, he has a plan. He asks three questions:

- What are we doing that you like?
- What things would you like to see us do that we are not doing?
- What things are we doing that you would like to see us do better?
  (Coaches corner 1993)

So what has he discovered so far? He says their customers like their people, but find them slow and not as responsive as they want. He goes on to add that their customers complain that AT&T does not give their people enough accountability or decision-making power to do what needs to be done. Customers want to work with people to make the correct decisions for their business needs. Customers want representatives to know more about their (the customers') businesses (Coaches corner 1993). Can there be any doubt about what is near and dear to this CEO's heart? Such commitment to change is rare. Even more rare is the ability to sustain the effort.

## RULE #3: CREATE DISCIPLES/FOLLOWERS

An old adage says "it's easier to change *people* than to *change* people." People can be forced to change, but change will not change them unless they accept the change as good. Leaders of change should openly communicate with their people. Explain the value of the change and especially tell them what is in it for them. Explain the impact of the proposed change on the company. Keep the focus on the issues with an open two-way flow. There must be opportunity for feedback on alternative ways. Communication works best if both sides are prepared to be flexible and willing to modify thinking and plans. Develop final solutions after gathering preliminary information, not before it has been gathered.

A fun way to build commitments for a change and at the same time help your people think through this process that will be involved is by taking them through *storyboarding* (see Exercise #9). This exercise helps your people to visualize what impact the change may have and keep them in the "moment of truth" that always comes with every innovation.

---

## RULE #4: MEASURE AND MONITOR "IT"

---

One of the more popular training courses for executives consists of survival team-building exercises. Executives who have gone through this training sometimes strongly believe it has had a significant impact on their behavior. Many believe it was a great learning experience. But one study after another shows that it has almost no impact on behavior. A year later they are still behaving the same old way. They may believe they have changed, but no one else does.

All too often change is assumed to be working, but in fact is not working. An essential element to successful innovation is outcome measurement. If there is no measurable change, you can try another approach before much resources and time are wasted. Obviously, when it comes to establishing measurements, make sure to measure the right things (for example, measure quality, not the number of people attending quality meetings). Perhaps just as important, maybe more important, is ownership of those measures of performance. Have employees become actively involved in creating their own measurement and numbers systems. Encourage them to create incentives for positive behavior and disincentives for negative behavior.

## "JUST DO IT"

Successful innovation demands forethought. The bigger the change, the more forethought that is needed. Creating a good atmosphere for new innovations involves reducing inhibitors of change (Stock 1993). It is natural for people to resist change, but you can diminish this resistance by creating **dissatisfaction with the status quo**. Begin the process of change by finding out about your people, and about their feelings toward the status quo.

As previously noted, people get comfortable with the status quo. The reason you want to find out about their dissatisfaction is that people must have some dissatisfaction with the status quo before they can accept an innovation. Oh, they can be forced to change, but they will not support it unless there is significant pain associated with the old ways. Those people who feel pain with old ways are the ones most likely wanting change. Your first positive action when implementing innovations will be to clarify how much pain exists with the old ways of doing things.

---

**RULE #5: CREATE DISSATISFACTION WITH THE STATUS QUO**

---

If you believe dissatisfaction with the status quo is low, examine the results, gather additional information if you need it, and then share information that helps to create greater dissatisfaction. For instance, in doing additional research, you may discover a certain percentage of your customers choose a competitor because of certain on-the-job behaviors. You may also discover market share is being eroded because of poor service. In either case, share and clarify the pain of remaining with the status quo. If you find out that 20 percent of your orders are late, or some cost is greater than a competitor, then let others know about the situation.

Gathering and sharing any qualitative data that supports the need to innovate is an essential prerequisite to change. Some examples of information you might share about the current status quo includes having (1) too much work to do in the current work situation, (2) no available method or procedures for doing a better job, (3) no recognition system for doing work properly, (4) inadequate rewards, and (5) inadequate tools or equipment (Stock 1993). Bryon Stock emphasizes that status quo conditions like these or others can be used to raise the level of dissatisfaction. When the perceived level of pain is great, people will be more receptive to innovation. However, this does not mean your goal is to try to create fear. There is already plenty of that in most change situations.

# FEAR

Many people still resist anything new even if they are dissatisfied with the status quo because they fear change. Fear may not be logical, rational, nor reasonable, but it does inhibit any innovation. The best defenses against fear are information and patience. William Bridges writes about human change in life and work, and describes three phases of change. He calls them the ending, the neutral zone, and the beginning (Iacovini 1993). If you want to successfully implement innovations, you have to help people work through these phases. When you try to implement the innovation, one of the first impressions you may get is a sense of frustration because many do not see the benefits of change. Doing something different is, for some, like standing at the edge of a dark chasm. They are told to jump—but to where? There is often an overwhelming frustration because the old ways no longer work.

The fear for some is even worse because they do not even talk of change, at least not openly. Everybody knows there will be changes, but few managers rarely discuss it, nor clearly understand how the change personally affects them or their people. Under these conditions, it is natural for people to resist giving up old habits, attitudes, and roles. It is not that hard to understand why they are afraid. Work and what we do often help to define us as a person, and make us feel useful and important. No one wants to lose the comfort zones and personal identity they have built up over years. Despite our protest, we like the status quo.

W. Edwards Deming said that driving fear out of the workplace is more important to continuous improvement than all the cherished statistical techniques of total quality control (Iacovini 1993). Employees and managers will let go, people will change, but there needs to be a sense of trust, dialogue, and negotiation. Reducing fear is possible but, unfortunately, managers compound natural fears of change by discouraging discussion of such issues. When we want to implement a change, there is a tendency to perceive struggles as unwanted and unwarranted resistance to a new or creative alternative. We tend to want to straighten out troublemakers and that is the wrong approach.

Straightening out people will not work, but there are several things you can do to help people deal with the natural apprehension and fear of change. John Iacovini identified several of these including the following:

- Give your people visible support.
- Try to point out areas that will remain stable and will not change.
- Give your people an opportunity to informally interact and share information and feelings.
- Use the past rather than ignoring it, and try to build on those accomplishments.
- Try to be sensitive to the fact that different people are at different stages of accepting the change.
- Counsel people and help them identify what they are holding on to, and most importantly, why.
- Focus on being supportive for your people in letting go of old ways of doing business.
- Constantly give information on the change, and just as importantly, give them a safety net when they make mistakes.

Try to keep people focused on the rational thoughts rather than emotional fears. Remember, people often hold on to old ways, even if they are not productive ones. Even if change is desired, many will be afraid of it. Many people would rather be safe above anything else, even if the current situation is not productive or satisfying.

Getting some people through what John Iacovini calls an impasse will take some work. He says overcoming this impasse is similar to getting your car stuck in the snow. If you gun your engine and spin your tires, you just get stuck even deeper. On the other hand, if you slow the engine and gently rock the car back and forth, momentum will eventually allow you to move forward (Iacovini 1993).

Like inexperienced drivers stuck in the snow, if an organization tends to rush through this resistance or this impasse stage, people can get psychologically stuck and roll back into old patterns. That is why it is up to management to realign people who are at an impasse. Iacovini suggests when an organization or person reaches an impasse you should do the following:

- *Take time* to look at where things are.
- Try to *encourage creative thinking* and tolerate diversity.
- Encourage people to *reflect on the past* and think in new ways about the future.
- *Focus on feelings* and exploring new ideas.

Iacovini's advice may reduce fear, but until the change is better understood, resistance will still remain strong.

## RULE #6: VISUALIZE A FUTURE STATE

Chapter 12 noted the importance of clearly defining your vision. Fear alone is never enough to make people want to change. Supporting a new innovation is unlikely unless our people perceive this new future as having fewer obstacles and more benefits than the status quo. Experts like Warner Burke, among others, emphasize that a prerequisite for leading change is to **create a vision of the future state.** The difficulty of this task has already been noted. It takes time to get together to discuss the future; nevertheless, paint a clear picture of the future. You must be able to describe tasks or activities that will be easier or better under the new change. When you better articulate this future state, the change will be more easily accepted. Before articulating this vision, *listen* for ideas. Before saying that change is needed, first ask participants how they can, or would, improve the process.

Listening alone can provide you with much information, not only about what people fear, but also about what they like about the old ways of doing work. You can also find out what good relationships or collaboration already exist, then describe how the new innovation can improve or strengthen these relationships. Try to build on the similarity to the current situation, identify what positive values exist in the old, and show how the new innovation will strengthen or reinforce what was good.

## RULE #7: TELL PEOPLE WHAT IS IN IT FOR THEM

The ideal situation involving a new innovative technology or work arrangement is for all those involved to have a complete understanding of the change and have a positive consensus about what the future state will be after the change. In reality, it will take continuous effort to fill in just the important parts. For each of us, the important parts and important information is the stuff that directly affects us. People do not need, and often do not care about, all the details of a new change, but the details directly affecting them will need to be well thought out and articulated.

We all see the benefits of change differently. Any change for many will still be resisted, even when there is dissatisfaction with the status quo. It will be resisted even if you have done your best to clarify the future state. The reason that some still resist is that they do not see the *positive outcomes of change.* In other words, they want to know "what's in it for me?" They want proof that the change will be personally good for them. You can show the advantages of change by telling success stories, by making visits, discussing it, and promoting testimonials. One especially powerful technique for showing the advantages is to use pilot studies or projects (see chapter 14). In the end, though, much will depend on your own willingness and personal efforts to promote the new innovations.

## WHAT DO YOU WANT?

When we talk of change we often underestimate the time, energy, and emotion involved in overcoming inertia. Executives sometimes seem to believe that creating a new product, process, or service is more important than implementing it. Many executives perhaps feel more comfortable developing creative solutions than in dealing with the human side. For whatever reason, change can fail if it primarily consists of a splashy presentation, a printed document, and nothing else (Koehler 1992).

| RULE #8: DEFINE THE RESULTS YOU WANT |
| --- |

Larry A. Huston is the manager of total quality for Procter and Gamble's worldwide research-and-development program. He talks of the need for visualization, which involves management understanding an innovation's strategic intent, then consistently and continually reinforcing it throughout the organization.

Visualization is more than talk. Not only are you creating a vision of the future that the change brings, but you make sure necessary resources are allocated to the change. It means you are going to need clear and *definable objectives* if you are to avoid simply spinning your tires. Center your people on what needs to be done by specifically defining what profit, market share, or volume you expect from the new change; otherwise, they will be confused about what is expected, and what they are to do. Most importantly, once you have decided on a specific objective, say like a 25 percent market share, then define how to do it. Only then would it be wise to plan and deploy your resources.

## TYING COMPENSATION TO CHANGE

Many innovations in the past failed because management did not have the insight to change the reward and recognition criteria. Why install a new quality improvement system but not change the evaluation system? Author Preston G. Smith points out that one of his clients had a strong dual-ladder system in which technical and managerial employees had equal advancement opportunities. However, the company decided to start emphasizing self-managed teams, so there is a need to consider a third ladder for team leaders. To do otherwise would make it difficult to convince talented people on the managerial or technical ladder to lead teams (Smith 1993).

Only when a reward system is in place is it wise to assign accountabilities and check the results. The effort should be on identifying barriers blocking more effective performance. At Procter and Gamble, for instance, they have several aims for their assessment process including: (1) assessing both the results and quality of those results, (2) assessing the capabilities of the organization, and (3) achieving greater organization alignment (with your objectives) (Koehler, 1992).

## JUST-A-LITTLE-LATE TRAINING

Once your objective setting and evaluation system is in place, you are finally ready for change. Some changes can occur immediately, but long-term change itself cannot occur without a great deal of training. You do not need to train everybody all at once, but you do need to commit your best people to the change process and prepare them to change.

Training is only needed when people must do things differently than before. Most managers know that some training is needed for implementing a change. Some of these same people recognize that it is the quality, not the quantity, of the training that is critical. However, fewer are aware of the fact that it is the sequence and timing of training that are essential.

Training is perishable. If you do not use it, you lose it. Preparing people for change and explaining new roles are useless unless they occur just-in-time or even just-a-little-late. Time and money will be wasted if several months pass between the time of the training and when it is used. People must feel that training is pertinent. There must be a strong interest in learning new skills for training to *stick*. The solution is to offer training just before it will be needed. It might be even better if people have had a chance to struggle a bit before introducing training.

# SUMMARY

A study conducted by a Harvard Business School team headed by Michael Beer noted the futility of expecting outside or staff experts to successfully implement change. The team looked at a number of large-scale corporate change programs. Some succeeded, while others failed. What they discovered was that, when company-wide change programs were installed by staff groups, they did not succeed (Schaffer 1992).

Successful innovation requires that members of an organization's change efforts focus on the details on how to implement change at the operational level. It requires showing how the current and past change efforts are doing. If managers are in fact thinking of making a change, they should also get an idea of what resources will be needed for those efforts to be successful. In other words, lead the change, do not just react or resist it.

Know what you want to change. If you are unsure what to change, you might consider doing a needs assessment. Once you have decided *it*—what you want to change—then plan it out and make sure you are focusing everything around that concept so everyone is trying to change the same *it*. Spend most of your time creating buy-in and trust, dealing with fear, and developing a core of disciples who are the true believers in the new order of things. Finally, do not assume. Just because it should work or feels like it is working, it may not be reality. Test reality. See how *it* measures up and correct if necessary. Remember *it* probably will need correcting.

# REFERENCES

Coaches corner. 1993. *NCR News* (November/December): 2 (in-house publication).

Hiner, Glen H. 1994. *Corporate change to face the challenges of global competition.* Presentation at 'Cadena Del Exito 1940,' an executive meeting hosted by S. A. Vitro in Monterrey, Mexico, 11 February, 4.

Iacovini, John. 1993. The human side of organization change. *Training & Development* (January): 65–66.

Koehler, Kenneth G. 1992. Effective change implementation. *CMA Magazine* (June): 34.

Schaffer, Robert H., and Harvey A. Thomson. 1992. Successful change programs begin with results. *Harvard Business Review* (January/February): 80–89.

Smith, Preston G. 1993. Why change is hard. *Across The Board* (January/February): 55.

Stock, Byron A. 1993. Leading small-scale change. *Training & Development* (February): 45.

# CHAPTER 14

# Techniques and Exercises for Innovation

## INTRODUCTION

This chapter contains several interactive exercises. Section I, Exercises 1–4, help you personally improve your innovative thinking. Section II helps an individual, group, department, or organization find their zone of creativity. Section III deals with how to implement innovations so they have the best chance of success.

## SECTION I—FINDING YOUR CREATIVE ZONE

### EXERCISE #1 "MIND MAPPING"

This exercise helps groups visually *see* their main problem and how one problem leads to another problem or consideration. The purpose is to fully explore the problem and its interconnections. It is good to begin a creative process because it helps to lay out the parameter of a problem.

---

**EXERCISE #1**
Mind Mapping

A central idea is drawn in the shape of a circle or square. New ideas are drawn in the form of spokes branching from this central idea. It is meant to visually help develop connections between ideas that might not otherwise be seen (Couger, Lynn, and Hellyer 1994).

Mind mapping was created by Toney Buzan of the Learning Methods Group in England. It was based on research that showed the brain worked primarily with key concepts in an interrelated and integrated manner. To begin the process of mind mapping, write the name as a brief description of a problem in the center of a piece of paper and draw a circle around it. Now brainstorm each major component of the problem and draw lines outward from the circle. You can even draw branches from these initial *roads* as you brainstorm more detail. It often helps to draw each line of inquiry with a different color. You can brainstorm all the lines at once and the branches for each. Another approach is to brainstorm a complete road or line of thought before moving on to the next line of inquiry. It is not uncommon to branch out and discover related topics. Mind mapping not only helps to encourage creativity, but it is also good in helping you explore *all* issues and subissues related to a problem as well as their pros and cons

---

# EXERCISE #2 "MANAGEMENT-BY-THE-FUNDAMENTAL QUESTION"

This exercise can be used with groups, departments, functional areas, or entire organization. It is designed to help people get on the same wavelength. Have the group begin discussions about who they are. Have them agree on a definition of what you are trying to accomplish and how you are going to go about doing it. This is an ongoing activity that helps keep people focused on the goal of the organization. The rationale for this exercise is that it is impossible to produce good improvements and innovations if you do not know what you are trying to improve.

---

**EXERCISE #2**
Defining "Who You Are"

Management-by-the-fundamental question (MBFQ) is a mental exercise, as seen in Figure 14.1, that is best done in a small group. It begins by asking ourselves to define "who we are." Each step should be agreed upon and openly discussed.

**EXERCISE #2**
Management-by-the-Fundamental Question

**What do we want to change?**

→   Who are we? (definition)

→   Where are we going?
(strategy, mission)

→   What do we do?
(assessment of customer satisfaction; make money)

→   Why do we do it?
(reflection)

→   How do we do it?
(activities, policies, procedures, methods)

→   How are we doing?
(measures income statement, market share)

→   How can we improve?
(training, and so on)

Figure 14.1.

# EXERCISE #3
# "FORMULATING CREATIVE SOLUTIONS"

This exercise is designed to get creative efforts focused on the right area. The first step is to ask general open-ended questions followed by more specific ones. Finally, this exercise concludes with closed questions that should help you identify the exact nature of the problem. A summary page is provided that gives general advice for attitudes that both encourage and inhibit creativity.

**EXERCISE #3**
Formulating Creative Solutions

Problem statements are means to ends, not the ends themselves. Often a problem statement will not lead directly to a good solution but rather will lead to another problem statement that will produce a breakthrough. It is impossible to tell which problem statement will lead to the best solution; we should try to generate as many statements of the problem as possible, without evaluating them. The more statements, the greater the likelihood that one of them will lead to a creative solution. The key question to continually ask is "What are you trying to solve" or "What is our purpose?" The following is a series of questioning exercises that can help bring out creative solutions.

**EXERCISE #3**
Discovering the Problem
(Probing Sequence)

A probing sequence involves asking a series of questions to gain sufficient information to identify what solutions are needed. Probing questions should be used to get more details, examples, and clarification.

The probing sequence can be depicted as a funnel as seen in Figure 14.2. You first ask yourself or a group a very *general open question.* Your objective is to encourage plenty of leeway in a response.

Your next step is to follow up the key points you discovered by asking a more *specific open question.* Continue asking specific open questions until you feel you have received all the information you need, or have discovered the underlying issues that need solutions.

Your final step is to ask a *closed question* to verify if your conclusions are accurate. If they prove to be incorrect, begin again with a general open question.

**EXAMPLE OF A PROBING SEQUENCE**

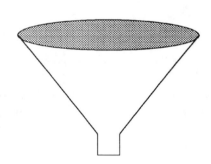

**\* General Open Question:**

"What problems are we having with the process?"

**\*Specific Open Question (Probe):**

"What was the problem with that step?"

**\* Closed Question:**

"So did the light come on when the machine stopped?"

Figure 14.2.

**EXERCISE #3**
Listening Naively Helps People Think Creatively

| WHAT ENCOURAGES CREATIVITY | WHAT PREVENTS CREATIVITY |
| --- | --- |
| Putting yourself in their shoes. | Staying with your preconceived ideas. |
| Assuming you know nothing about what solution is needed. | Assuming that you know what is best because you are the expert or have done it this way and it has always worked. |
| Actively trying to understand what people are saying. | Hearing what you want to hear. |
| Asking *dumb* questions. | Assuming you ought to know the solution already. |
| Wanting to listen. | Taking the attitude that you will *listen* if you must. |
| Being open to suggestions. | Pushing your agenda or ideas. |
| Checking out the conditions that caused the problem. | Assuming you know the cause of the problem. |
| Involving everyone in listening (everyone in the process). | Being very directive. |
| Providing quick feedback and acting on what you have heard. | Infrequent, slow, and irrelevant feedback. |

**Figure 14.2.**
**Continued**

# EXERCISE #4 "DISCUSSION 66"

This exercise is a quick approach for getting people to focus their creative efforts. It is usually given after the team or group has decided what problem needs the most creative solutions.

---

**EXERCISE #4**
Discussion 66

Don Phillips, former president of Michigan's Hillsdale College, developed a technique known as Discussion 66. A small group of six members includes a leader and a reporter. A single problem is assigned to each group, and a solution must be reached in six minutes. After the reporter has recorded the solution, the group is given another problem to discuss. At the end, all recorded solutions are sent to decision-makers (Creative Group Techniques 1984). It works well for minor problems or large ones that are broken into small digestible pieces.

---

# SECTION II—ASSESSING YOUR CREATIVITY

# EXERCISE #5 "THE INNOVATIVE IQ SURVEY"

This exercise is designed to help you identify the amount of creative and innovative thinking occurring with your group or organization and compares that to demands expected from your environment. The form that is included shows the categories and related questionnaires. Figure 14.5 also provides a way of graphing the responses. To request copies of the original copyrighted version or to get more sophisticated analysis of the questionnaire, please contact:

Dr. D. Keith Denton or Dr. Peter Richardson
Department of Management
Southwest Missouri State University
901 S. National
Springfield, MO 65804
or
call Denton 417-836-5573
or
Richardson 417-836-5575

**EXERCISE #5**
Your Innovative IQ Survey

This survey tool helps describe how well your organization seems adapted to its business environment as well as helps clarify the degree of rigidity or ability to respond to changes in your environment. It can also be used to suggest potential strengths, weaknesses, and overall competitiveness in terms of adapting to changes in your competition, customer expectation, cost, and other outside forces that affect your business environment.

- Helps identify how well your organization or parts of it seem to be well adapted to your competitive and business environment.
- Identifies the organization stability and degree of resistance to innovation.
- Examines your culture and helps you identify if it is appropriate for your current marketplace.
- Describes the degree of dynamic change existing both within the company and in your business environment to see if they are appropriate.
- Identifies the likelihood that your organization will be able to respond to changes within your business environment.
- Determines the degree of change within your business environment and compares that with your company's profile to see if you are in tune with those changes.
- Helps determine how well you are prepared to respond to changes in your customer expectations, changes in your overhead and cost structure, technological changes, and your primary competition moves.
- Provides you with graphical pictures that give a profile of the rigidity and flexibility within you or your organization and compares it to the change occurring within your business environment.

The questionnaire should be given to your group or organization. Have members fill out the questionnaire (Form 1) (see Figure 14.3). They should record their answers on the attached *scoring sheet* (see Figure 14.4), then take the average of those responses and record them on the *creative index* (see Figure 14.5). Responses will show if your organization is responding in a creative manner. Compare that to your environment. Questions A through F assess the creativity within your organization. Questions G through L determine the amount of change and uncertainty existing with your environment. The greater the uncertainty, the greater the need for innovative practices. If responses are generally "below the zone" but your environment is one of instability and change, then consider increasing creativity and decreasing rigidity.

*Copyright D. Keith Denton and Peter Richardson* (used with permission)

**EXERCISE #5**
The Innovation IQ Survey ©
Form 1

Organizational Factors

This 12-subject questionnaire is designed to survey a wide range of attributes involving change. It can indicate a wide range of strengths and weaknesses. The questionnaire can be filled out by you, your superior, or your subordinate. These can then be used to compare perceptions, and so indicate areas for improvement.

**INSTRUCTIONS:** Read the following questions, then circle the response that most accurately describes your feeling: Strongly Disagree, Moderately Disagree, Mildly Disagree, Neither Agree Nor Disagree, Mildly Agree, Moderately Agree, or Strongly Agree. If any of these questions *do not apply to your situation* or if you simply *do not have enough information* to make a decision, then circle *Don't Know or Cannot Say*.

**BACKGROUND INFORMATION:**

COMPANY _____

CHECK THE ONE BOX THAT MOST CLEARLY DESCRIBES YOUR POSITION:

☐ Top management (CEO, plant manager, president, vice president)
☐ Middle management (department head, division chief, and so on)
☐ First-level management (line supervisors, and so on)
☐ Staff position without supervisory responsibility
☐ Nonmanagement

### A. Divergent/Lateral Thinking

1. In this organization we are encouraged to think in different or contrary ways, challenge traditional assumptions and bring in as many different perspectives as possible.
2. In this organization we are nontraditional, if it works we do it with little regard for rules, rituals or what was considered proper behavior in the past.
3. People at the top of our organization do not act alike, they have diversified views and behaviors.
4. Our organization's culture exposes people to other perspectives rather than just one way of getting things done.
5. People in this organization are encouraged to explore new behaviors and actions in order to resolve problems.
6. In this organization, people are moved around to different jobs so we can be exposed to different parts of the organization.

**Figure 14.3.**

## B. Information / Idea Flow

7. Our organization focuses more on improving lines of communication rather than following lines of authority.

8. Throughout this organization, we pretty much operate without a lot of clear-cut bosses; most think of themselves as part of a team rather than as subordinates.

9. It is easy to communicate horizontally (across, back and forth and among departments and functions).

10. Information about what is really going on within the organization is readily shared at all levels, either through formal or informal means.

11. In this organization, people are free to ask any question they wish. Nothing, except personal or medical information, is off-limits.

12. Feedback in this organization is given rapidly and frequently rather than just relying on quarterly or annual feedback.

13. When people find and share ideas with others, they are often praised or recognized in some way.

## C. Flexibility of Control

14. Management spends most of their time clarifying who we are and where we are going rather than managing the details of how we do it.

15. Management sets the targets and leaves the details to employees.

16. In this organization, it is the situation, not the boss, that defines what needs to be done.

17. In this organization, there are very few sign-offs and review procedures before decisions are made.

18. Teams within the organization generally operate autonomously or self-directed rather than being told what to do.

19. Rather than being told what to do, in my job, I pretty much figure it out for myself.

20. We do about the same things most of the time, but we rarely do it exactly the same from one time to the next.

## D. Risk-Aversion / Taking Tendencies

21. In this organization, we tend to make decisions that challenge the status quo.

22. This organization is open to risk and does not perceive new methods, procedures, and information as threatening.

23. This organization is not afraid to risk some failures in order to try new things or look for new solutions to problems.

**Figure 14.3.
Continued**

*(Continued)*

24. Our unit spends at least 5 percent of our work week trying to improve, enhance, or develop new methods, procedures, products, or services that increase our competitiveness or profitability.

### E. Responsiveness to Change

25. A formal 3- to 5-year strategic plan about where we are headed does NOT play a very large role in my work unit's ability to make decisions or changes to deal with new or unexpected situations.

26. The organization would be more likely to accept new ventures or opportunities that required it to change the way it is set up and run, rather than to turn it down so that we don't have to change the way we do things.

27. In this organization, decisions are generally reached quickly rather than going through a long, deliberative process.

28. This organization is very flexible about how things get done rather than following lots of standard operating procedures, rules, or regulations.

29. This organization tends to respond rapidly to new market trends, product and technological development, or service innovations.

30. In this organization, concerns of the customer are dealt with in a variety of ways, tailored to fit the situation as opposed to using standard procedures or approaches uniformly applied to all situations.

31. We try to deal with our customers' needs by anticipating them rather than waiting for customers/clients/constituents to bring them to our attention.

### F. Adversity and Creativity

32. In this organization there are high expectations about work performance.

33. Our organization expects sudden dramatic improvements in performance as opposed to the gradual incremental changes.

34. Our organization operates to meet the standards of our pickiest customer rather than our average or typical client.

35. Rather than benchmarking against our direct competition, we benchmark against the best there is in our type of business.

### G. Changes in Consumers' Expectations

36. Our customers always seem to be expecting increasingly faster response time.

37. Our customers always seem to be expecting better quality.

38. We would lose customers if our competition improved its quality.

39. Our customers always seem to be expecting us to constantly lower our cost.

40. We would lose customers if our competition lowered their prices.

41. Our market share is likely to experience significant increases or decreases in the next few years.

**Figure 14.3.**
**Continued**

42. Rather than having a mostly stable and unchanging customer base, we are constantly losing some customers and gaining others.

43. Individuals or organizations that comprise our customer base are likely to change significantly in the next few years.

44. Our customers' needs always seem to be significantly changing.

45. In order to remain competitive in the next few years we will need to seek out new niches, products, or services.

46. Our customers are increasingly demanding customizing so that they have more options or service to choose from.

## H. Changes in Competition

*47. Our primary competitor's demand or sales have been increasing faster than ours.

*48. Our market share has not been going up or down in direct relationship to our industry's growth rate. (Our share tends to either increase or decrease slower or faster than the industry growth rate.)

49. Our competition in the next few years is likely to increase significantly.

50. In our line of business, old competitors seem to be always falling by the wayside.

51. In our line of business, new competitors or rivals are always emerging.

52. Our competitors always seem to be changing what they do or how they do it in order to improve their competitiveness.

53. In our market, it's winner take all. It is more like open warfare rather than live and let live.

54. We think of ourselves as competing with the best in the global marketplace rather than primarily competing with local competitors.

## I. Cost Changes

55. The profits we are able to make from each product or service we provide can vary greatly.

56. We are in a constant state of trying to reduce the cost of our resources.

57. Our cost of capital always seems to be changing.

58. Our pricing and distribution costs are always changing.

59. The costs of our raw materials and supplies are subject to significant changes.

*60. There is little direct relationship between increases or decreases in our demands and corresponding increases or decreases in our profits.

*61. There is little direct relationship between our current assets and our current liability.

**Figure 14.3.**
**Continued**

*(Continued)*

*62. There is little direct relationship between increases or decreases in our net income and corresponding increases or decreases in total assets.

*63. There is little direct relationship between increases or decreases in our cost of goods we sell and corresponding increases or decreases in the average amount of inventory we have.

### J. Labor Changes

64. The size, cost, and availability of a competent labor pool with the skills we need greatly fluctuates from one year to the next.

65. Our workforce experiences significant turnover.

66. Our workforce experiences significant absenteeism.

### K. Technological Changes

67. In our type of business, technological changes and revolutions are always occurring.

68. Technological changes, in the near future, are likely to have a strong effect on our business.

69. Our product development times or time needed to bring new services on line will need to continue to reduce.

### L. Global Forces

70. Changes in the tax policies, interest rates, and money supply have a significant impact on our organization's strategic or long-term actions.

71. Changes in tax policies, interest rates, and money supply have a significant impact on our organizational day-to-day operational activities.

72. Our organization is significantly impacted by changes in, or formation of, governmental trade agreements.

73. Fluctuations in the stock market have a significant impact on our business.

74. Our organization is significantly impacted by changes in, or formation of, government regulations.

75. Our organization is significantly impacted by the state of the economy of other countries.

*These questions, unlike the others in sections G through L, are not opinion but rather are facts. They are ratios that can be calculated and, as such, are more likely to represent reality rather than opinion. Ratios like these are the basis for "phase planes" like those seen in chapter 11.

**Figure 14.3.**
**Continued**

Environmental Compatibility Survey ©
Form 1 Scoring Sheet

This survey is designed to collect opinions about a wide range of characteristics of your organization and the environment in which it operates. It can be filled out by you, your supervisor, or subordinate.

**Instructions**: Read the following questions on the survey and then circle the response on this sheet that most accurately describes your opinion ranging from Strongly Disagree, Moderately Disagree, Mildly Disagree, Neither Agree Nor Disagree, Mildly Agree, Moderately Agree, Strongly Agree, or *if you do not have enough information or cannot say, then circle "Don't Know or Cannot Say."*

|  | Strongly Disagree | Moderately Disagree | Mildly Disagree | Neither Agree Nor Disagree | Mildly Agree | Moderately Agree | Strongly Agree | Don't Know or Cannot Say |
|---|---|---|---|---|---|---|---|---|
| 1. | 1 | 2 | 3 | 4 | 5 | 6 | 7 | CS |
| 2. | 1 | 2 | 3 | 4 | 5 | 6 | 7 | CS |
| 3. | 1 | 2 | 3 | 4 | 5 | 6 | 7 | CS |
| 4. | 1 | 2 | 3 | 4 | 5 | 6 | 7 | CS |
| 5. | 1 | 2 | 3 | 4 | 5 | 6 | 7 | CS |
| 6. | 1 | 2 | 3 | 4 | 5 | 6 | 7 | CS |
| 7. | 1 | 2 | 3 | 4 | 5 | 6 | 7 | CS |
| 8. | 1 | 2 | 3 | 4 | 5 | 6 | 7 | CS |
| 9. | 1 | 2 | 3 | 4 | 5 | 6 | 7 | CS |
| 10. | 1 | 2 | 3 | 4 | 5 | 6 | 7 | CS |

**Figure 14.4.**

## Creativity Index©

Plot the results from Figure 14.3 on Figure 14.4. Average each of the categories from the questionnaire and plot those means on Figure 14.4. Categories A through F are designed to assess the creative climate at work. The more people are encouraged to use lateral and divergent thinking (A); the better the flow of ideas and information (B); the more flexible the control process (C); the more risk taking (D); and more responsive to change (E); the more creativity potential that exists. Category F is based on the belief that high standards create stress that ultimately leads to innovative approaches.

These categories should then be compared to categories G through L, which essentially assess the degree of stability and lack of change that exist in your marketplace. Scores below four (4) means you work in a very stable environment where there is less need for creativity and more emphasis on repetition and predictability.

### CHAOS AND RANDOM DISORDER

| | | YOUR ORGANIZATION | | | | | | YOUR ENVIRONMENT | | | | | |
|---|---|---|---|---|---|---|---|---|---|---|---|---|---|
| | | A | B | C | D | E | F | G | H | I | J | K | L |
| | | Divergent/Lateral Thinking (Av. 1–6) | Information/Idea Flow (Av. 7–13) | Flexibility of Control (Av. 14–20) | Risk-Aversion/Taking Tendencies (Av. 21–24) | Responsiveness to Change (Av. 25–31) | Adversity and Creativity (Av. 32–35) | Changes in Consumers' Expectations (Av. 36–46) | Changes in Competition (Av. 47–54) | Cost Changes (Av. 55–63) | Labor Changes (Av. 64–66) | Technological Changes (Av. 67–69) | Global Forces (Av. 70–75) |
| In the Creativity Zone | 7 | | | | | | | | | | | | |
| | 6 | | | | | | | | | | | | |
| | 5 | | | | | | | | | | | | |
| | 4 | | | | | | | | | | | | |
| Below the Zone | 3 | | | | | | | | | | | | |
| | 2 | | | | | | | | | | | | |
| | 1 | | | | | | | | | | | | |

**Figure 14.5.**

# SECTION III: IMPLEMENTING INNOVATIONS
## EXERCISE #6 "DOS AND DON'TS OF CHANGE"

This exercise can be used by groups, departments, or organizations to walk them through the change process. Specifically, it is designed to get everyone thinking about how best to implement innovations. In particular, it forces people to assess both their good and bad experiences with implementing change and then encourages them to draw up an action plan to follow.

---

**EXERCISE #6**
Dos and Don'ts of Change

Have people follow steps A through G of Figure 14.6 and follow the appropriate instructions. The goal should be to get everyone thinking about how to effectively implement changes and innovations.

A. Individually, "Think of a situation in which you responded *negatively* to a change at work that was suggested or implemented by someone else." List those factors of the situation that made you respond negatively. Focus on *how the change was suggested or carried out* rather than the change itself.
(10 minutes)

B. "Now think of a situation where you responded *positively* to a change at work that was suggested or implemented by someone else." Then list factors that made you respond favorably.
(5 minutes)

C. As a subgroup share the information each of you has listed. Select a recorder to summarize and record your team's responses (will report to entire group).
(10 minutes)

D. Discuss, summarize, and record (as an entire group).
(15 minutes)

E. Develop *guidelines for suggesting and implementing change in a way that creates a positive response to change* and then record on an inventory for all to see.
(10–15 minutes)

F. As a reassembled subgroup, create an *action plan* so your subgroup can implement a specific plan. Select a recorder and record and present plan.
(15 minutes)

G. Reconvene the full group—each group presents entire *action plans.*
(15 minutes)

---

**Figure 14.6.**

# EXERCISE #7 "HOW TO INTRODUCE CHANGE—A SEVEN-STEP EXERCISE"

The first parts in this exercise are designed to get people thinking about how to successfully change. This is a more directive approach that recommends a specific sequence of activities. A more compressed form for fleshing out this sequence is also provided.

---

**EXERCISE #7**
How to Introduce Change—A Seven-Step Exercise

The following exercise will enhance your ability to successfully implement change. It is a seven-step process. Forms for this process are provided (see Figure 14.7).

Step 1. *Define the status quo and its background.* Anytime you want to make an innovation, you can begin by defining the current state-of-affairs. Note the relevant background surrounding the present situation. State relevant facts and activities that help identify a problem. Review previous actions or thoughts that have already been considered, but primarily focus on defining the results by using the following process.

Step 2. *Establish a "problem statement."* To formulate a concise action statement, it is critical to begin with the words *how to.* Include an action verb (for example, something that shows movement) that describes what is to be done, what outcome is expected, and when. These statements should answer the question how much and how soon.

Step 3. *Brainstorm.* By opening up the problem-solving process by seeking the thoughts, wishes, suggestions, and recommendations on how to solve the problem you have defined.

Step 4. *Select ideas.* Select an idea or ideas by prioritizing those that hold the greatest potential for improvement.

Step 5. *Analyze each idea's benefits/concerns.* Analyzing potential benefits and concerns about the most promising ideas is the next step. Try to develop at least three benefits first, then and only then list any concerns that might prevent success. Concerns should be framed in the form of *how to* statements. This sequence helps prevent potentially good ideas from being killed prematurely.

Step 6. *Overcoming concerns.* Minimize concerns mentioned in step 5 by stating them as potential problems. Concerns should be started as *how to* or *I wish* statements. The reason for this procedure is so these concerns can be recycled through the sequence of steps as a new problem that can be overcome.

---

## Forms for
## "A SEVEN-STEP PROCESS FOR INTRODUCING CHANGE"

*Step 1.* Define current situation (be as specific as possible). _____

Note relevant background information _____

State any relevant facts _____

Note any prior actions (or thoughts) already considered _____
Define results desired _____


*Step 2.* Problem statement.
We want to determine, "How to _____

What is to be done _____

What outcome is expected _____

When are results expected _____


*Step 3.* *Brainstorm ideas.*

1. _____   4. _____
2. _____   5. _____
3. _____   6. _____

*Step 4.* Select ideas (which ones hold the greatest potential for improvement).

1. _____
2. _____
3. _____

*Step 5.* Analyzing potential benefits/concerns

Idea #1: _____

Benefit (#1) _____
Benefit (#2) _____
Benefit (#3) _____
Other benefits _____
Concerns for Idea #1: _____
(1) "How to. . . _____
_____

**Figure 14.7.**
**Form 1**

*(Continued)*

163

```
        (2) "How to. . . _____

    _____

Step 6.  Overcoming concerns.
         Concern for Idea #1 - "How to. . . _____
         Concern for Idea #2 - "How to. . . _____
         Concern for Idea #3 - "How to. . . _____
         Other concerns—"I wish. . . _____

Step 7.  Create an action plan.
         Who will do what? _____
         By when? _____
         How will we know it's been accomplished? _____
         When will everyone get back together? _____
```

**Figure 14.7.**
**Continued**

# EXERCISE #8 "PLAYING CARDS FOR CHANGE"

This exercise is as open-ended as the exercise is rigid. It asks participants to deal out cards with covers similar to those in Figure 14.8. The purpose is to encourage discussions of how best to implement change in their situation. Participants are asked to decide the best sequence of events and fill in blank areas that are not on the cards. It is a fun and useful way to get group discussion when members' experience with change is fairly limited. It also makes a good icebreaker for many groups and helps everyone start thinking in the same sequence.

---

**EXERCISE #8**
Playing Cards for Change

Cut out playing-sized cards with descriptions glued to them similar to those shown in Figure 14.8. Make sure numbers are not included. Also cut out a couple of blank cards. Ask the group to arrange the cards in the correct sequence. They have been arranged here around three concepts (Decide, Do, and Review). Have the group reach agreement on what should come first, second, and so on, and then report the result to a larger group.

The exact sequence is not as important as the consensus-building discussion that revolves around the activity. Having a couple of blank cards allows the group to explore unique constraints or conditions within their area. The activity should take at least 30 minutes and a follow-up presentation can take another 20 to 30 minutes.

Create a large chart and give it to each member who can then use it as a guideline for future meetings and activities.

---

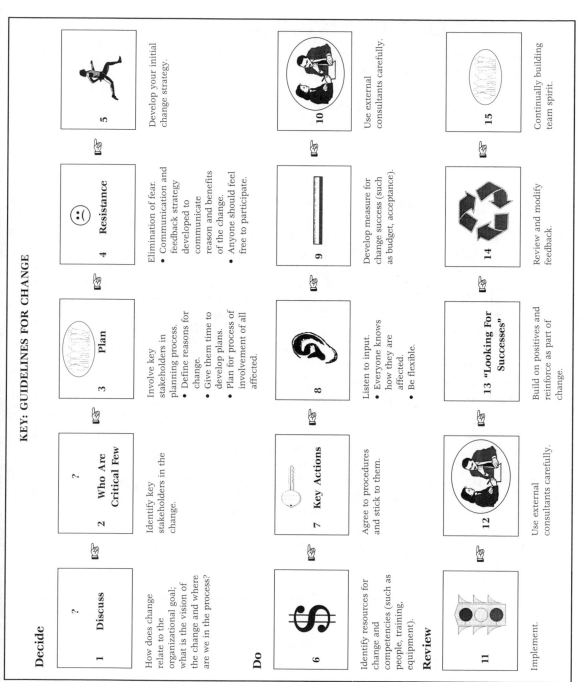

Figure 14.8.

# EXERCISE #9 "STORYBOARDING"

This is another visual tool for helping groups, departments, or whole organizations focus on the key steps to successful implementation. Some areas where it might be used are seen in Figure 14.9 and the sequence of steps are seen in Figure 14.9. The participants can draw their own storyboard (Figure 14.10) or use some of the attached graphics included in Figure 14.11.

---

**EXERCISE #9**

"Storyboarding": Visualizing the Future

Children love to visualize the future in their pictures and painting. Audi, in their 1996 Annual Report, showed some pictures of children who were concerned about polluting automobiles. Their pictures show cars driven by wind-power, muscle-power instead of petrol or ingenious magnetic systems that automatically take cars to their destination. Children readily give free rein to their creativity, without worrying about practical matters. They don't ask—"Will it really work?" "Is it technically possible?" or "Is it affordable?" This is how new ideas come into being (Annual Report 1996). That is the purpose of storyboards. The idea is to use cartoons to express creative concepts or resolve problems in an original way.

With yourself or a group, identify a situation that needs innovative or creative approaches. Some potential ones are seen in Figure 14.9. These are only suggestions, many others are possible. Next, assume you are to create a 30- to 60-second videotape where you will do four things. These steps are seen in Figure 14.9 and include: defining the change you want, describing the exact situation or thing you want to change by finding a "moment of truth" where conflict will arise over this change. Using this moment, create your storyboard. This is done by breaking down the major scenes and using either sketches or graphics that are provided (see Figure 14.10) to create a visual picture of the sequence of events. Storyboarding helps you visualize success and helps you think through the key steps essential to your success. It can be used by one person, but works best with two people or a very small group. Use your own drawing skills (stick figures are nice) or use some of the graphics that are attached to create a novel or original approach to your problem (see Figure 14.11).

---

Defining The Situation To Be Storyboarded

*Conflict or situations might involve things like:*

- Not continually keeping up with the competition.
- Team members not helping out and working together.
- A few people left to do all the work.
- Someone not doing their part or not being dependable.
- Personality clashes.
- The team not performing well.
- The team's "drifting" without direction.
- Meetings that don't seem to accomplish anything.
- There is little or no effective communication.
- No planning or not enough of it.

*You are to create a 30- to 60-second "videotape." In it you will:*

1. *Define* the change you want to implement (10 minutes)

2. *Describe* as detailed as you can the exact situation or event that is critical to this change. Visualize a *moment of truth* at some point in the future where a *conflict* will arise over the change. Using this conflict or situation as a central theme, create your storyboard about how you would respond with the new innovation you have implemented. Some ideas you might storyboard are attached.

3. First, break the event down into *major scenes* and work out what might be said and how it will be handled. Next, after you have worked out the actions, either sketch, or use paste-up decals that are provided to you to visually show what is occurring. Do this last step only after you have worked out the details about an event and how it will be handled!

4. If you are working in a group, then bring your storyboard back to the entire group, have someone act as a facilitator to describe or *act out* the scenes of your storyboard so we can all envision how you would react in this future conflict.

**Figure 14.9.**

STORYBOARDING

Describe scene: _____
What's going on: _____
Key actions: _____

**Directions:** Identify 9 to 12 important or major scenes.

**Description:** A storyboard should show a rough sketch or picture of some key activity (can use some materials we supply). Each picture or scene should contain a caption that:

- describes the scene
- identifies what is going on
- briefly highlights the actions and communication that is occurring in the scene.

Figure 14.10.

Figure 14.11.

# SECTION IV—MISCELLANEOUS
## EXERCISE #10 "INTRODUCING INNOVATIONS USING PROJECT TEAMS"

This is advice directly from someone who has successfully implemented change through project teams. It includes steps for building a good team.

---

**EXERCISE #10**
Introducing Innovations Using Project Teams

David DeVowe, the manufacturing technology manager at Tool Product Company in Minneapolis, says that you never introduce a new concept to the whole organization, rather you should pilot test everything. All of their pilot projects consist only of volunteers. The idea is to build as much success as possible for the new innovation. Tool Products also found it beneficial to erect invisible barriers between their old (traditional) system and their pilot teams so there was no direct reporting relationships and no interference.

DeVowe also mentions that the company found it useful to create a core group of action takers and visionaries that kept their team development process fast paced and moving forward. Finding this group of go-getters would be essential to creating early success and gaining experience with streamlining decisions. Along the same lines, the company also found it was more effective to create their own internal leaders rather than an outside guru (even though they did make use of some outside help).

### Pilot Test Everything

Tool Products found it effective when the *project team generated their own numbers*. It was not so much a matter of what was being measured as it was having the group create their own numbers so they had a sense of ownership about those numbers. Feedback on performance, as well as measurement, was important. David DeVowe said visual communication boards were extremely effective communication tools.

Finally, Tool Products found that innovations can only occur with good education. They, like other companies, found it necessary to use education as a means to nurture the innovation. In particular, they applied education in parallel with the change just in time to shore up any exposed weakness. Exercises in this section are designed to help your group develop the sense of ownership essential to successful innovation.

Many companies that have experience with change, use an exercise to get across key points. The exercise involves paper planes. In order to teach team members of the importance of communication, GE sets up assembly lines for making paper airplanes. Each person makes a fold and passes it on. The only rule is people can't talk to each other. At the end, the planes are flight tested. As you can imagine, many don't fly. After emphasizing the need to share information, the group does the airplane exercise again. This time they can talk to each other. Guess what—the planes fly! The point is: Teamwork is important whether you're making quality paper airplanes, quality refrigerators, or anything else. Innovations are most likely to work if information about the process is actively exchanged and conflicts resolved among those affected by the change. The seven-step process for introducing innovation (see Exercise #7) can often be used with this exercise.

## Building a Good Team

Frequently, project teams do not go as smoothly. Reasons can stem from a lack of understanding of the importance of each member. One way of developing this appreciation is to go through the following exercise with your group (adopted from Ford Motor Company's *We Are a Team* 1988, 16).

Step 1.  Each member chooses the same job or task within your group and spends about 30 minutes preparing a brief statement of:

(1) What does this task involve?

(2) How does it affect others in the group?

(3) How does it contribute to the group's performance?

Each person then prepares similar statements about their own role and responsibilities as well as how their work affects and is affected by others. (A less time-consuming alternative to focusing on one function at a time is to have each person just do this last step of focusing on their role. However, recognize that if the idea is to create a better working relationship then choosing common functions to discuss is a good idea.)

Step 2.  Statements prepared in step 1 should be verbally discussed within the group to make sure each person has a clear understanding of what everyone does and its implications to the whole team.

Step 3.  Next make two lists. The first is called *expectations* and the other is called *commitments*. Both are statements of actions needed to improve the efficiency of the team. In the case of expectations, it is a list of actions you need from others. Commitments would be what you would be willing to do to improve the process.

Step 4.  Now, verbally exchange these expectations and commitments with the rest of the group. This is the point where a great deal of discussion should occur. The purpose is to clarify and understand what is needed to improve your chances of success. Finally, this discussion should be followed by written agreements made by each person stating what they will do for the group. Each person should also receive a copy of the agreement. Follow-up meetings should be scheduled to check on progress and to focus on implementing the innovations.

# REFERENCES

Annual Report for Audi. 1996, 29.

Couger, Daniel, Patrick Lynn, and Doris Hellyer. 1994. "Enhancing the creativity of reengineering." *Information Systems Management* (spring): 26.

Creative group techniques: Part 2—Alternatives to brainstorming. 1984. *Small Business Report.* (October).

*We Are a Team.* 1988. Ford Motor Company Booklet, 16.

# INDEX